398

S0-CWS-951

# the treasury o

# puppies

Judy de Casembroot

OCTOPUS BOOKS

First published in Great Britain in 1973 by
Octopus Books Limited
59 Grosvenor Street, London, W.1.

© 1972 Octopus Books Limited

ISBN 0 7064 0085 2

Produced by Mandarin Publishers Limited
77a Marble Road, North Point, Hong Kong.
Printed in Hong Kong

# Contents

# Buying a puppy

Doctor John Brown (1810–82) wrote: 'I think that every family should have a dog. It's like having a perpetual baby. It's the plaything and crony of the whole house. It keeps them young.'

This is certainly very true, a dog in the house does help to keep you young and it takes you out as it must have exercise. It keeps you young not only in body but in mind too, since through it you will make friends and thereby exchange ideas. Your children will enjoy the companionship of a dog enormously and they can be taught how to love and care for a dog at an early age. This will stand them in good stead when they grow up, to say nothing of the happiness it will bring them when they are young.

There is a very important point which must be made right at the beginning and that is that you should not decide to have a puppy or any kind of live-stock unless you are prepared to devote some time and trouble to it. The buying of a puppy is a most important milestone in your family life and should not be undertaken lightly. Great thought should be given as to what breed you buy. If you live in the town, with not much space in which to exercise your pet, then you

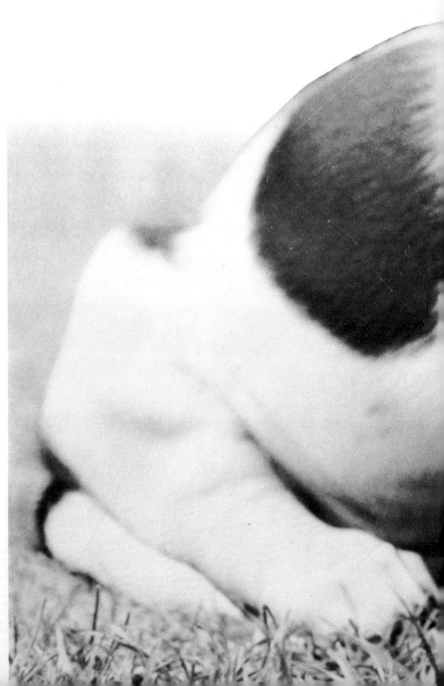

*A Basset Hound puppy living up to the reputation of the breed of being the clowns of the dog world with a marked ability of playing to the gallery. Although these dogs are now extremely popular as pets, they are working dogs and pack animals, and there are still several packs which go out regularly after hares. Not being fast, they eventually run their quarry to ground through excellent nose work and persistence. Bassets have the most beautiful hound music of all the hounds, and it is well worth going to see and hear a pack of Bassets as they are very different from the rather idle, clown-like characters that are the domestic pets.*

should choose a breed that is of the smaller variety. The family may have ideas of a big guard dog, such as a Great Dane, an Alsatian, or a Doberman, and there are many other breeds of the same size, but unless you have the space in which to let them gallop about, and the time in which to exercise them, do confine your ideas to a dog which will fit in with your way of life. The long coated breeds require grooming at least three times a week and bathing during certain times of the year. You will also have to ensure that he has no livestock such as fleas or lice. Above all you will have to make arrangements for him to be regularly fed when you go away, even for a short time.

It is essential you and your family understand that a puppy requires almost the same sort of attention as a baby. He requires the same regular meal times with almost the same frequency. He must have regular times when he can attend to the calls of nature. He must be provided with toys with which to play. He requires rest periods in which to sleep and grow. He must not be a plaything for the children all day long. The children must be taught that a puppy needs love and care just as they do. He should also have a certain amount of discipline, as without some training he can become a nuisance not only to you but also to your friends.

From the very first day he becomes part of the household he must be taught your way of life. He must be taught to stay alone, which will be a difficult lesson to learn as he has been used to his brothers and sisters to keep him company. This is a very important first lesson and you must be firm about it. He may be very pathetic and appealing and it is so easy to give way in the beginning, but like the baby he knows just how long he must cry in order to get the attention he craves. Once you have

*Left, a Beagle puppy, almost a puppy no longer.*

*Opposite, Dalmatian puppies. These dogs were used to follow carriages in the old days and love going out following a bicycle or a horse.*

*Above, yellow Labradors playing in the scrub.*

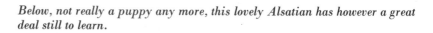

*Right, an old English Sheepdog just three months old.*

*Below, not really a puppy any more, this lovely Alsatian has however a great deal still to learn.*

*Left, this Afghan Hound puppy is a magnificent specimen and although delightfully modest he is obviously aware of his striking appearance. Above, Pekinese make devoted pets.*

given in it is fatal and you will be one of those dog owners who can never go out or go away unless you have a baby sitter or, shall we say, a dog sitter, since even a small puppy can make a great deal of noise. Therefore it is essential he learns from the day you have him that he cannot always go everywhere with you.

The second lesson, which is also time consuming and sometimes difficult, is house training. This also has to be taught at the start of your partnership with him. It does take somewhat longer than the first one

and there will be many mistakes before he is finally clean in the house. Like a baby, his needs are little and often, and he cannot be expected to go through the night without interruption. However by following the methods suggested in this book, he will learn in time, but do be patient and take trouble to help him.

The third lesson is to teach him to be obedient. Ideally he should come when you call him, sit and remain in his basket when you tell him to do so, walk quietly on a collar and lead, and stand still when you want to brush and comb him. He should allow you to groom him without snapping or fidgeting about, which spoilt dogs so often do. If you do not insist on this when he is young, grooming, which is such a necessary part of his life, can be a source of trouble to you all his life. The long coated dog soon learns

if his owner is going to give up brushing him when he snaps, so do not choose one with a heavy coat which requires 'combing' as well as brushing if you are not prepared to spend time accustoming him to being groomed. All the time and trouble you spend on your puppy while he is a baby will be time well spent as it will pay dividends in developing his character and when he is fully grown. He will give you years of devotion and companionship, and fun and pleasure to all the family.

Love him and pet him but do not on any account spoil him. A spoilt undisciplined puppy can grow up into a treacherous savage adult and a danger to you and your family. This is especially true in the case of the larger breeds. That little puppy snarl which can be so funny in a baby puppy can turn into a nasty bite when he

13

grows up, so be prepared to take trouble in his early training. When you say 'No' say it firmly and stick to it. There is no need to be unkind, just be firm.

A puppy is at his most receptive to learning between the ages of five weeks and three months. It is at this early age that he first becomes conscious of the human being, and it is essential that nothing should happen to give him cause for distrust at this early age. Breeders should do all they can to 'socialize' their puppies at this point. They should get used to being handled and talked to by people. They should be brought into the house for a period each day, which will get them used to the household noises, such as radios, banging doors, telephone bells, tradesmen and strange people. This is essential if any of the litter are to be sold as house pets. It is unlikely all will develop into show dogs, but this early training will help in their show careers as well. It is an established fact that puppies which have the advantage of a family life from birth are much firmer in temperament than a litter born in a kennel, leading a sheltered life with no experience of the sights and noises of a household. They get used to one voice, which is most likely a woman's, and are then cared for at first in their new home by a woman so they tend to be afraid of men. Of course in most cases they grow out of this but it can have a lasting effect. This is especially so among those breeds which show the disposition to become very attached to one person in the household. It is also a fact that when a puppy is sent by rail or taken by car to its new home (this also applies to the older dog) it will attach itself to the first person that either takes it out of the basket at the station or has the first contact with it on arrival in the car. Many puppies are a bit apprehensive at first in a new environment and it is a most interesting fact that they will show no fright and go happily to the person they have first met even at an early age.

The last and very essential part of the future care of the puppy for the would-be dog owner is *exercise*. It is most important that time should be devoted *every day* to this. While the puppy is aged from two months to five or six months the confines of a garden are quite sufficient for the smaller breeds such as Toys, Terriers and Cocker Spaniels. The bigger breeds however, unless the garden is, say, the size of a tennis court, should have somewhere in which they can have a free gallop to extend their limbs and help them to grow. Games with a ball can give the puppy and you great fun, no matter what the breed.

It is most important to realize that the bigger breeds must have adequate exercise. The 'tennis court' size of garden is sufficient for the big breeds whilst they are up to six months old, provided they have free access to it. After this age it is most important you are able to take them somewhere where they can have their freedom. They should not be walked on lead before they are six months old. Many of the large breeds such as Afghans, Pyreneans, Alsatians, Dobermans, Boxers, Great Danes and Setters are now very popular and they all require a great deal of proper exercise when they are adult. In the event of your being unable to provide this necessary exercise, do choose one of the smaller breeds. They can be just as lovely a pet and companion. A big dog deprived of the right kind of exercise and freedom can be a misery to himself and your family. He has no outlet in which to express himself, and perhaps one day he bites and so he is labelled as 'savage'. Basically he is not savage at all, only bewildered. He is full of pent up energy and had he been properly exercised, he would never have bitten in the first place.

Any dog just like a child with nothing to do becomes bored. Boredom can lead to mischief, and this can then lead to your puppy becoming a problem dog. The mischievous antics of a puppy which make you and your friends laugh may not be the cause for laughter when he grows up. A playful nibble at the carpet edge when only a few weeks old does not do much damage. However, later on you may return home one day to find

*St Bernard puppies will need careful rearing, as do all the large breed puppies.*

the whole carpet in shreds or he may have amused himself by tearing your cushions to pieces. The result of this little activity is most aggravating, down or feathers being the most difficult things to clear up. This was discovered by a dog owner who had left her pet in a hotel bedroom. Having made short work of her underwear he went to town on the eiderdown. The scene which met her was a nightmare and her reception when she went to report to the management extremely chilly.

Such a thing can happen in the best regulated circles and with the best behaved dog who has had plenty of exercise, but it is less likely to occur with a well-trained animal who has been taught to behave himself when he is left alone. The culprit in the above incident was a 'Kennel dog' and had received no training other than walking on a lead in a show ring.

The owner was really extremely foolish leaving him free in a hotel bedroom and thereby paid the penalty for her lack of training and 'socializing' of him as a puppy.

Lastly you will have to remember that owning any animal can be a tie to your family activities. This especially applies to a dog and in particular to a puppy. Like a baby he will require feeding, little and often at first, so you must therefore be on hand yourself or arrange for someone else to do this for you. In order that his house training does not suffer, he must be let out after each meal or else he may turn into a 'sooner' dog, which is one that would sooner oblige in the house than in the garden. Many a puppy has been nick-named 'Sooner' owing to this bad habit, which is difficult to eradicate once it has been allowed to creep in in puppyhood.

You will probably have to train him to travelling in a car, and some take to it from the first, while others suffer from car sickness as do children. Patience can overcome this. Actually the eight weeks puppy is generally a good traveller, it is the older puppy that suffers from this distressing complaint.

Having gone into all the details 'against' having a dog at all, let us consider the 'fors', and they are legion. The only mistake the good Lord made was not to have made the span of a dog's life the same as man's.

However short the life of a dog is compared to ours, all the trouble you may have to go through to train him, all the worries you will encounter when you have to nurse him through his various ailments both as a puppy and an adult, are worth every moment of stress, for the joy and endless happiness he will bring. As a companion and friend for young and old alike the dog has no rival. They are entirely unselfish, their cheerfulness is so infectious, their continual energy so stimulating. Whatever you do, you are always right in the eyes of your dog. Nobody else thinks you are perfect except your dog.

When he goes, as go he must, nothing and nobody can rob you of the memories of owning him. At first it will be heartbreak and sorrow, but then you will remember with thanks and gratitude all the happiness he brought you in his life. Those frantic greetings of delight at your return when you had been away if only for a day. You will remember a thousand

and one joyous moments and be able to take comfort from the thought that you gave him a happy life and equipped him well to enjoy his all too short a span.

*A heart to love you till you die,*
*That's a thing that money can buy*

*A look of love from a loving eye,*
*That's a thing that money can buy*

*A tongue that will never tell a lie,*
*That's a thing that money can buy*

*Ear and tongue, and heart and eye*
*That's a thing that money can buy*

*Wherever dogs are offered for sale*
*These are the things that money can buy.*

*Left, Welsh Springer Spaniels at play. These make most attractive pets as well as being excellent gun dogs if properly trained at the right age. Right, a happy Cocker Spaniel puppy raring to go. This is a lovely puppy, but not in fact a very good show specimen as he is too broad between the ears. The three Cockers (below), on the other hand, are of excellent pedigree and look as if they are well aware of the fact.*

# Choosing a puppy

The great day has come and you have finally decided you want to have a dog in the household. It is important that all the family are agreed that they want one. The children will undoubtedly have been clamouring for one for months past, and no doubt their father is in agreement, but it is on mother's shoulders that the responsibility is going to fall and it is essential that she is a real animal lover and wants the worry and care of a puppy too. Among all her many chores, hers will be the task of seeing it is fed at regular times and taken out for its walk. At first the children will want to help, but once the novelty has worn off, which regrettably it does quite quickly, mother will be left to cope, so unless she loves dogs and will really welcome the extra burden added to her already crowded day, do not buy a puppy.

A dog is regarded as a puppy up to the age of six months and until recently a licence was not compulsory until this age. However under more recent legislation, a licence is required from the moment you acquire it, no matter what the age. It is important, therefore, that you decide beforehand what age puppy you want. Ideally the best age is two to three months. Never on any account buy one before it is aged eight weeks. There are many breeders and books that will tell you that a six-week-old puppy is old enough to face life in a

new home. This may be so in some cases and some puppies of this tender age may thrive and do well. You are, however, taking a great chance in one so young. They are only just weaned and should anything go wrong, such as unsuitable food, a chill, even a change of water (this can cause upset tummies) you can have a very sick puppy on your hands. At this age they have not the strong resistance to a change of circumstances that they have at eight weeks. This two weeks may seem a very short period, but it can make all the difference, as that extra time can build up their resistance and constitution. Therefore no matter how sweet the puppy or persuasive the breeder, do not be persuaded to buy .any puppy before the age of eight weeks.

It is an accepted fact that the gradual weaning of puppies starts at about three to four weeks of age. The breeder generally starts to get the puppies to lap or take a small quantity of scraped raw meat at about this age according to the size of the litter and ability of the mother to feed them. The whole process is very gradual, covering a period of a couple of weeks. However, the mother has still been attending to the puppies. night and morning, and they have had the comfort of her presence. If you really think about it, and realize she has been their way of life, their comfort and solace up to this time, six weeks of age is much too soon to take them away to be completely on their own, in what to them is a cold unfriendly world.

There are of course lots of puppies which may be weaned completely by the age of five to six weeks for a

variety of reasons. Maybe it has been a large litter and their mother has not had sufficient milk to feed them longer than five or even four weeks; consequently they are used to feeding on artificial food. However they still remain together as a litter. They have the warmth and comfort of their brothers and sisters and the security of life so essential to the very young. They play together and live together as a single unit. To take one away suddenly at the early age of six weeks is taking a chance that its future may be affected by the shock of the sudden change.

You may have decided you do not want the worry of such a very young puppy in which case three months is the next best age. Unfortunately breeders want to sell their puppies as soon as possible, puppy rearing being a costly business, and it may not be easy to find an older one, or if you do, it may be the least attractive of the litter and consequently been left to the last. If you are buying from a kennel, do not purchase any puppy between the ages of six and eight months. The reason for this being that they are now used to the routine of kennel life. Of course there are, as previously stated, exceptions to every rule and you may get one of this age that settles down at once. However, there is a chance he may not.

Another and important factor is character. He will have already formed certain ways which may not fit in with your ideas of dog behaviour. You will also miss the best part of his puppyhood, plus the fact that the small puppy is much easier to train than the 'teenager' to which the older puppy could be likened. It may well be you are not able to care for a tiny puppy in which case be very sure that the temperament is good in the older puppy. At the above ages he should have been taught to walk on a collar and lead and have a pet name to which he will respond.

From four and a half months upwards he will be in a difficult teething period, as at this time he is cutting his double teeth. This can cause him to be nervous with strangers, and it is not a good age to change from a kennel life to a household pet.

If circumstances dictate you must have an older puppy, try to get one of eight to nine months of age, but be prepared to pay more for it in consequence. Remember also it may not fit into your household at all happily

*Above, Bloodhound puppies look as solemn and sad as the full grown dogs, though their wrinkles are not so voluminous.*

*Opposite, Borzoi puppies. These are Russian hounds with a very aristocratic appearance and affectionate natures.*

*Left, Pyrenean Mountain pups with a Siamese cat as their companion. Below, a Beagle pup eyes his handsome companion rather dubiously.*
*Right, a Lhasa Apso pup with a Colourpoint kitten. These were Tibetan watch dogs and from their honey-coloured coat and courageous possessiveness they get their name of 'Little Lion Dog'.*

at first. You will have to be prepared to be patient and get him used to all the strange ways of a house and all the household noises he never encountered in a kennel. He may have a delightful character and be full of confidence when you collect him at the kennels and he may get in the car with you quite happily and then when you get him home, will suddenly take fright and disappear under the nearest sofa. You may have been lulled into a false security by his friendly actions at the kennels and let him off the lead, in which case he will disappear into the nearest woods or dash off down your garden path into the road and be hit by a passing car.

A true story is told of a red Cocker Spaniel sold at eight months to a home where he appeared to be quite happy and free from any nerves at all. He had been in his new home for ten days and had been off the lead for about three days, when in the garden one evening at dusk just as he was being brought into the hall, somebody dropped something which made a great clatter just in front of him. He at once darted back into the drive and disappeared. No amount of calling would induce him to come into the house, and as darkness fell there was no sign of him. The police were informed and so were the breeders, who luckily lived not far away.

Fortunately most lost dogs remain in the area unless they are chased or frightened off. This proved to be true in this case, the puppy was frequently seen round about, but nothing and nobody could persuade him to be caught or return to the house where he had given every indication of being content. Several times he was seen and the breeders notified but by the time they were able to get to the spot he had vanished again.

It was not until three weeks later that he was finally caught by the breeder who was well versed in the ways of dogs. She piled several Cockers into her car and drove to where he had been seen last. Then remaining in the car, she let all the Cockers out, who took off up the road with much barking and noise. At once a little red foxlike figure appeared from the woods and stood poised for flight. It was a tense moment and had the breeder got out of the car it is certain the wanderer would have fled. However, on seeing only the dogs he waited for them to reach him, and the recognition was instant and the reunion a joy to see.

He remained quite happily in his new home from that day onwards and lived to a ripe old age. So be sure and keep you new dog on a lead for at least two weeks when away from the security and confines of your house.

This all really leads back to the idea of having a puppy of two to three months old. There is no doubt that he will settle down at once, except perhaps for a few days protest at night when left alone. He loves everyone and has no reason to fear life at all.

However, what is even better is that you should have two puppies. If your pocket and your home can cope with two this is the ideal arrangement. They keep each other company: they play games together and they grow together. What is more you have no trouble when they are left alone when you want to go out, so you are not conscience stricken when you creep out and hear a little complain-

ing voice. Of course a single puppy will soon learn to be on his own, if you are firm, but at the same time there is no doubt that two will be company and you will be more independent.

They must, however, be the same sex if you want them as pets. Your friends may try and persuade you to have two unrelated and breed puppies to make some money but it does not work out that way. The female will always come in season at the wrong time. You cannot keep them together during this trying period – one or other will have to go into kennels, an expensive item for you and probably an unhappy time for whichever one you decide to board. Dogs hate being sent to board even in the best organized kennels. Many are complete these days with radio and curtains at the windows. Your pet, however, would rather be out in the rain in a ditch with you than in the cosiest and best boarding kennels without you.

Deciding on which sex you want can always be a subject for discussion. Most families want a male thinking it will be less trouble than the female. Some, it is true do have a roaming habit, but this need not be so if they are properly exercised. Neither is it necessary or advisable that they should be provided with a mate during their lifetime. The pet dog very often has no idea what is expected of him when presented with a 'lady in an interesting condition'.

In the event of your having de-

cided to have a male as your pet, do not let him wander at will. Do not be tempted just to let him out in the garden and jump the wall to go off on his own, thinking to yourself he will come back, because it may be that one day he will not. First of all he could get run over and secondly he could develop wandering habits and thereby become a nuisance to you and a menace to the neighbourhood.

Dogs may become wanderers not only through force of circumstances, but also through their natural instincts. They want to be with you and share your life, but if you neglect them, they will go off for walks on their own, and will even do this in order to draw attention to themselves at home. Therefore if you have a male, look after him and exercise him well, and if you have chosen one of the larger breeds be sure the exercise is adequate for his size and breed. It is essential that the larger breeds should also have a certain amount of discipline. They must be taught to be obedient from the time they are very small. You may choose one of the big breeds because you want to have a guard dog, but if he is kept pent up and short of freedom, or teased or spoilt by your children, he may show the threatening attitudes towards you that you would prefer him to show to unwelcome strangers.

A small puppy can grow into a big unmanageable adult, who, unless you give him training as a puppy, may turn on you or your family through sheer frustration. Unfortunately this

*A family of Staffordshire Bull Terriers.*

often happens and is one of the reasons why many of the big breed clubs have started what they call their 'Rescue Service'. They have organized a system among their breeders whereby one of them will undertake to rescue an unwanted puppy that has proved to be a problem child to its owners. They will collect it from its home, sometimes with difficulty, try to restrain it and finally find it a new home with more suitable conditions.

It is generally the bigger breeds that have to be re-housed as people do not think when they buy the puppy. So many purchasers go to a puppy farm, where all breeds of puppies are for sale. They see an attractive, furry one and fall for it without having any idea of its ultimate size or what it may cost to feed when it is an adult. Many of these big breeds are very attractive when they are small, such as Pyrenean Mountain Dogs, and the Golden Retriever is another that looks just like a little teddy bear as a puppy. The puppy farm owners are only interested in selling their stock and with many would-be owners walking round their kennels, they have no time to enquire into the future life of the puppies they sell. The result is that many purchasers go away with that small furry bundle, having no idea that it will grow into a dog weighing 100 to 125 pounds and standing anything from 25 to 32 inches at the shoulder, as in the case of the Pyrenean and many other breeds. So please find out the ultimate size of

your puppy before you buy it.

The ideal way to set about buying a puppy is to decide on what breed you want before you start out. It is important to remember that you are buying a live animal, that is going to share your life for anything from 10 to 14 years, or even longer in some cases, and you do want to know something about its background.

A good breeder and dog lover will also want to know if the prospective owners are going to be suitable owners. For this reason you should buy from a breeder. By doing this you will be able to see the adults of the breed of your choice, and most breeders will probably give you a diet sheet. They will tell you how much exercise the puppy should have. They will advise you as to grooming and inoculations. What is more you will have an after sales service from a reputable breeder, as they will be interested in the future of the puppy they sell. Their future livelihood depends on it, and they keep dogs in the first place because they love them. There can really be no other reason for keeping a kennel at all. Rearing, raising and training dogs is not all fun all the time. You have to be prepared to be on call 24 hours a day, and can never be certain of any free time. Would-be puppy owners tend to take a long time choosing their puppies, particularly if they bring a large family to help make the decision. A good dog breeder has to be dedicated and will be properly concerned that you should start with the right puppy, be it male or female.

You may decide to have a female, because the family think it would be nice to have a litter later on. There is nothing wrong with this idea, and it means that you can then keep one of her litter to take her place when she dies.

What are the disadvantages of keeping a female or bitch as the English kennel owners will call them? (They are referred to as male or female in America.) The first and foremost problem is her season. This is the period in which she becomes interesting to the opposite sex. It is a time when you will have to ensure that she is exercised only in the confines of your garden. It must be securely fenced with high wire, so that no would-be suitors can get access to her. At the correct time in her season she will be as anxious to get to them as they will be to get to her.

This first season generally appears from seven months onwards according to the breed. On no account should any breed be mated at this first period. Both male and female are able to conceive at this tender age, but it is not advisable. A story is told of a Smooth Fox Terrier aged eight months, kennelled in error with his grandmother, his mother and his aunt, all of them being in season. The result was a litter to all three, even though his time with them was a brief 48 hours. A Cocker Spaniel dog aged eight months mated a very willing bride aged 18 months, and the result was five puppies all of which did quite a lot of winning in the show ring. Which all goes to show that care has to be taken from an early age.

Females never develop the wandering habits of the male. Some will tell you they are more affectionate and easier to train than males, but really it is a matter of personal preference.

The problem of her 'season' is a real one which must be given thought before you make your final decision. It is essential that you have somewhere to exercise her in the garden during this period. She must not be taken for walks as she will lay a trail for all the male dogs in the district, and your garden will be besieged by them. This can be a nuisance to you and can wreck your garden too. The season lasts for three weeks, sometimes a little over, but the confines of the garden are quite sufficient for her. Some owners make use of a boarding kennel at these times, but this is costly. She would much rather remain with you and miss her daily walk than be shut up in a kennel among strange people, kind though they may be. Of course, if you live in a flat, she will have to be taken out in which case if you have a car pop her into it and do not take her walking until you are some distance away.

Far left, a West Highland White Terrier puppy eight weeks old.

Left, a Saluki puppy. This is one of the breeds that are very hard to recognize when they are young.

Below, a Welsh Corgi and her puppy. This is a Cardiganshire Corgi and is heavier than the more popular Pembrokeshire and has a long bushy tail, rather like a fox's brush.

It is possible to give her tablets during her season which will disguise her condition and can be given at frequent intervals during the day for the full three weeks. They really are effective and can be used with safety. As in the case of humans, there is a veterinary Pill which can be administered to stay the season altogether, thereby preventing her having puppies at all. However, there is still some risk attached to its use as not all react to it in the same way. It is therefore advisable, should you buy a female with the idea of one day breeding from her, that you take the extra trouble and use the tablets, just in case yours is the odd case that reacts badly to the Pill.

Just in case you have not had a bitch before, perhaps it should be added that she will come in season roughly at six monthly intervals. It is only when she is in season that she can be mated. The time that she is ready again varies, generally it is round about the tenth to the fifteenth day from the start of her season. It is essential that you make plans for the mating with the stud dog of your choice as soon as she shows signs of the first coloured discharge, as popular stud dogs get booked up. One of the many advantages of buying from a breeder is that he can advise you in

*Left, Whippet puppy playing. These dogs can be many different colours and are very sweet tempered, clean, and easy to groom.*
*Above right, Border Collies are captivating, but their charm should be resisted as they are not happy living as pets.*
*Below, a patient Irish Wolfhound bitch with her two quarrelsome pups.*

this matter and often help you with the sale of the puppies too. It is important to remember that you must keep your bitch away from other dogs, even after she has been mated. Should she get out she can be mated again with no trouble at all and should this happen within 24 hours of the first service she can conceive to both dogs.

It is a fact that many dog owners do not know how to get in touch with a breeder. It is quite a problem, they rarely advertise in the local papers though the pet shops and puppy farms invariably do. It must be remembered that these shops and farms have bought their stocks from a breeder in the first place, therefore by buying from them you are paying more for the puppy than if you bought it direct from the owner of the mother of the litter. Another important point is that it has already had one change of home and environment, and runs the risk of picking up disease from contact with other dogs and puppies, which will not be the case if you go to a breeder.

There are two dog papers available which are published every Friday – 'Our Dogs' and 'Dog World'. They have to be ordered from your newsagent as they are not readily available on the book stalls. In both these you will find advertisements of various kennels from which you can make a choice of breed. There are many kennels up and down the country and no doubt you would find one near you. 'Phone and make an appointment, don't just go on chance. Tell the breeder what you want. This is the best method of approach. If you want a really good looking dog, perhaps with show potential, say so. If it is only to be a pet, you will get an equally well reared one with some small show defect, which in no way detracts from him or her as your future companion.

Another way, and a very good one, is to contact your local vet and ask him to recommend some good kennels to you. He will have been attending the local dogs in your area, and getting to know him in advance would be an excellent thing for the future of your puppy too. He will be able to advise you in the treatment it will have to receive such as inoculations if the breeder has not attended to this before the sale. Your vet can indeed be a friend to you, so whilst you will enjoy reading the dog papers, contacting him first would be a most sensible thing to do.

Incidentally, if at any time you have to take your puppy to the vet's surgery, do not take him without ringing up and making an appointment. They all have surgery hours but it is not advisable to take a puppy into the surgery to wait, as he may come in contact with other dogs who may have an infectious complaint. This is very important in the early days of his life and in particular before he is inoculated. Either leave him in the car and go in yourself to wait your turn, or, if this is not possible, keep him on your knee and do not allow him near any of the other dogs which are waiting.

# Choice of breed

**W**hilst you may have firmly decided you are going to have a dog you may not be at all sure which breed would be best. There are so many to choose from that perhaps a few words on their various characteristics would help you to make your final decision. The place in which you live and the facilities you have for keeping any dog should really govern your final choice.

All gun dogs undoubtedly make excellent family pets. However they all, except perhaps the Cocker Spaniel, really require plenty of space in a nice big garden plus lots of country walks where they can run free.

The **SETTERS** are rumbustious and delightful dogs with boundless energy. As puppies they really do require three or four miles per day after the age of five to six months. You may only walk the four miles but with their high spirits and great enthusiasm they will double or even treble this distance by galloping round you in circles. Up to five months they do also need space in which to play.

**IRISH SETTERS** are really beautiful dogs. Their coats are a gleaming bright red almost the colour of a bright horse chestnut; being flat and glossy they do not require too much

*West Highland White Terriers are
cheerful dogs capable of great devotion,
very easy to keep and are thus
deservedly popular.*

grooming. They have delightful,
friendly characters, but need strict
training when young as they are so
full of life.

The **ENGLISH SETTER** comes in
three varieties of colours: black and
white, flecked all through and not in
patches, lemon and white and finally
tricolour, which is black, white and
tan. They too are most attractive and
handsome, not quite as wild as the
Irish perhaps, but still requiring the
same amount of exercise. They too
are very friendly, happy dogs and
both make lovely house dogs and are
excellent with children. Both are
about 25 to 27 inches in height when
fully grown.

The **POINTER** is another of the
gundogs which is a popular pet; he is
smooth coated so grooming is no
problem. He also comes in various
colours, lemon and white, orange and
white, black and white, liver and
white and tricolour, like his cousins
the Setters. He must have plenty of
free exercise, he grows to about 25 to
27 inches and as a puppy he has great
energy coupled with a very friendly
and happy nature. As adults they are
very attractive in appearance with
their clean cut lines and alert appearance.

You will certainly be attracted by
these three breeds, but unless you can
give them plenty of freedom it would
not be kind to keep one in the town.

**RETRIEVERS.** Whilst these too
need their walks every day they are
not quite as energetic as the breeds
previously described. The most popular are the Labrador and the Golden
Retriever. Both grow to about 22 to
24 inches when adult.

The **LABRADOR** is a most charming companion; short coated, his
colour is either black, yellow or liver.
He is a sturdy, well-built dog and
breeders have maintained his sporting instincts. Many sold as pets have
proved to be good gun dogs with a
minimum of training. Whilst he is
happy wherever you may live, he is
in his element in the country. Docile
and friendly in temperament, he is
good with children and makes a good
guard too, as he is generally naturally
obedient, given adequate training as
a puppy.

The **GOLDEN RETRIEVER** has a

very similar character. About the same size as the Labrador, he too is sturdily built with a golden or cream coloured coat, which is flat or wavy, but not short coated as with the Labrador. He has a very attractive head and expression. As a puppy he can really 'get' you as he is rather like a teddy bear, especially if he is cream coloured and has the appealing dark rims to his eyes. These dogs are very suitable for a family, liking both adults and children, but here again they ought to have country walks and freedom, though they do not seem to suffer in the same way as the Setters do from the lack of it. Both breeds are placid which may be due to their popularity; over the years more and more of them have gone into homes where they are the family pet rather than the family gundog. Fortunately many are still used for work and their sporting instincts have not been bred out of them. To see either breed at work is a great pleasure as they enjoy every moment doing what nature originally intended for them.

**SPANIELS.** There are now eight of these breeds with the addition of their cousin from overseas – the American Cocker Spaniel. The latter is a breed that has gained instant popularity by reason of its small size, (15 inches high,) and its outgoing and attractive personality. In the show ring this dog is a great extrovert as he has a fabulous long coat which flows along the ground as he flies round the ring. The crowd always applaud his performance with great enthusiasm. However, should you decide to have one as your pet, and the puppies certainly will attract you, do be prepared to spend a lot of time on his coat. It does need thorough grooming right down to the skin to keep him free from mats and tangles. His coat is really an adornment, but if it is matted and tangled, then all that can be done is to cut the knots out which will quite ruin his appearance. They are one of America's most popular breeds and you may well fall for one. But be prepared for coat problems.

**COCKER SPANIELS** are the most popular of all the spaniels – there are 18 Clubs for the breed and one of them has over 800 members. In one year just after the war their registra-

tions at the Kennel Club totalled over 27,000. Luckily they are now back to more realistic numbers, as over-popularity can ruin a breed, not only in character but in looks as well.

There is no doubt that as a pet the Cocker Spaniel is one of the best. Those who have had them as a pet say they will never have any other breed. Some of them also make excellent gundogs, but over the years it is as the household pet they have proved their worth. They have strong sturdy bodies, good bones and when adult should be about 15 to 16 inches high. Their coats do require attention at least three times a week. The groom-

ing should be thorough and the ears groomed with brush and comb right through. Particular attention should be paid to behind their ears, to the 'feathering' or long coat around the hind-quarters, and to under their forelegs. The hair can be cut back round their feet with scissors, so that they do not carry too much mud into the house. As the pictures will show they have charming heads and expressions. As characters and companions they are ideal family dogs, as long as you do not over-indulge them. They are very intelligent and soon learn how far they can go. They have developed a very strong guarding

*A family of 'Scotties'. These dogs have many admirers on both sides of the Atlantic.*

instinct and will often guard their possessions such as a bone or a toy. They can be jealous and sometimes attach themselves to one person in the household; should this be seen in puppyhood it should be firmly checked. They are also most susceptible to their owners – a highly strung owner will often have a highly strung dog, and although this applies to other breeds, it is most noticeable in the Cocker.

It is important when you go to choose a Cocker puppy from a litter that you avoid the one that hides in a corner and will not come to you. Choose the boldest and most friendly one. Your family may say 'Let's have the little shy one, it is so sweet', but do not be persuaded. Actually this may happen in other breeds too, so never choose a puppy that appears shy. It may only be a passing fright but on the other hand it may be an inherited fear and a frightened animal can become dangerous. Even a small puppy can give quite a painful bite. Therefore, if you have a choice, choose the bright and lively one.

The 'Seeing Eye' organization train dogs for the blind in America and do special tests for temperament on very young puppies in order to see their reactions to human beings. They put a lot of stress on the importance of early experience in a puppy's life. The special testers start the training at eight weeks, and then only once a week. The tests are started with simple commands such as sit, come, heel, fetch. The puppy is never punished or scolded if it does not obey, only the word 'No' is used; neither is he rewarded with food if he does well, only praise and petting. These tests go on for five weeks; if at the end of this time he does not retrieve, he will not be any use as a Guide Dog, as he will not be a willing worker. This does not mean he will not make a good companion dog. The

'Seeing Eye' in the States takes endless pains in this socializing of puppies. Cocker Spaniels in particular require human contact and handling from an early age. Left in a kennel too long, they do not accept life as a house dog as happily as some other breeds. They do not feel happy with small children at any age either if they have never encountered them. The best age to buy a Cocker Spaniel is between two and three months and if you rear him well and give him confidence you will not wish for a sweeter or more intelligent companion.

The other four Spaniel breeds are **SPRINGERS.** These are liver and white, black and white or tricolour. They are about 20 inches tall, and rather more racy in build than the Cocker Spaniel. They are gay companions, good shooting dogs, and easily kept as their coat is not as profuse as that of the Cocker. They would take more kindly to the free-

*Right, Shetland Sheepdogs almost fully grown, at four to five months, when they will be only 14 inches high. Left, a much younger pair of Shelties. Below, Tibetan Spaniels which are rather like the Pekinese only less exaggerated in both shape and coat.*

dom of the country rather than the restrictions of a town, but nevertheless are very adaptable. The same also applies to the **WELSH SPRINGER**, a somewhat smaller dog, beautifully marked with a bright red and white silky coat. He is not as forthcoming in temperament, but is a staunch companion and a good working Spaniel once he knows you. The **SUSSEX SPANIEL** and the **CLUMBER SPANIEL** are shorter on the leg with great substance in body, and are very friendly characters. The **CLUMBER** in particular with his large square head and lemon and white markings is a very attractive and lovable creature. He weighs about 60 pounds, whereas the Sussex is smaller and of a colour all his own – his coat is a rich golden liver shade and tipped with gold. Neither needs much walking. The **FIELD SPANIEL** is now gaining popularity again; he is an upstanding dog with a handsome head, standing 18 inches at the shoulders. He commands attention, is easily trained for work or as a pet, and good exercise is essential. Lastly, the **IRISH WATER SPANIELS** are spoken highly of and have a great sense of humour. They are the tallest of the Spaniels, stand-

ing 22 to 23 inches at the shoulder. They are a rich liver in colour and the coat is a profusion of tight crisp curls. They make splendid shooting dogs and companions. Should you live by the river or the sea they will be happy all day long. They are very active and energetic and would make an ideal present for a youngster who likes country pursuits.

There are 22 Terrier breeds; space therefore does not permit details of them all. The **AIREDALE** is the tallest of them all being 23 to 24 inches high. The rest are in the region of 18 inches to 10 inches. The Airedale makes an ideal guard dog and is a most handsome animal. His coat will need a certain amount of trimming which the breeder can advise you about. He must be taught obedience from the start, as Airedales are strong characters and need good handling. It would, therefore, be advisable to buy a young puppy and train it to your methods from the first.

**BULL TERRIERS** are great characters and very popular. They have a great sense of humour, are great fun as companion dogs and generally excellent with children. They have a

*Above, a family of Sussex Spaniels. Notice the broad heads. These Spaniels are a lovely golden liver colour, and do not need as much exercise as some of the other spaniels. Right, a nine month old Irish Setter. Following pages: top, the irresistible Cocker Spaniel puppy. Below, a family of 'Poms' is one that will be very hard to resist. Right, Boxer puppies.*

great deal of strength and muscle in their comparatively small frame, so you must control them from the start. Never allow them to pull on the lead, which they love to do. Whilst they will not go out of their way to pick a fight, they are full of life and very brave, so will not be averse to 'having a go', and it is for this reason that they must have strict discipline from their puppyhood.

Many of the other 20 Terriers are very popular.

**CAIRNS**, little shaggy dogs about 14 pounds in weight make admirable pets. They are fun to take out for a country walk and whilst they have quite a lot of coat it is easy to trim as

they cast it at certain times. They are very active and gay.

**SEALYHAMS, WEST HIGHLAND WHITE TERRIERS, FOX TERRIERS, LAKELAND** and **WELSH TERRIERS, SCOTTISH TERRIERS** with **NORFOLK** and **NORWICH TERRIERS** are all about the same size. Each breeder will tell you they all vary in character, and the last two do not require as much trimming as the others. The Norfolks have dropped ears, whilst the Norwich carry theirs erect giving them a very bright, expectant look. The other breeds on this list can always be trimmed for you at a pet shop or, of course, by your breeder.

The **BORDER TERRIER** has created a lot of enthusiasm just recently which is well deserved. With his Otter-shaped head and close fitting harsh coat, his sporting character and handy size he is ideal for many families and should be high on your list for consideration. He loves hunting whether it is rats or foxes, in fact he is so courageous he will take on anything, and yet is very gentle as a pet.

**BEDLINGTONS** too deserve a thought, as they were one of the original terriers dating back to 1750. Fashion has changed their shape now but they still have the same character and make good house pets. Their blue colour is most unusual and they are easy and clean in the house.

The **MANCHESTER TERRIER** is a smart dog with a smooth, jet black coat and bright tan markings. His size is right for the house, as he only stands 15 to 16 inches high. They used to be marvellous ratters, but there does not seem the opportunity for this sport now. It was fun in the old days when the farmer was threshing and the dogs all stood by expectantly waiting for the rats to run from the stack, and not many escaped.

With the loss of the rabbits there is very little sport for the Terriers now, but a little group of men have been seen busy with their ferrets recently. Ferrets and Terriers go together and

*Top left, a Cavalier King Charles Spaniel with her puppies.*
*Left, Dalmatian puppy playing with a lovely home-made toy.*
*Right, portrait of a Poodle pup.*

once the latter have learnt not to go after the former, ferreting is great fun, and maybe is coming back again as a country pursuit.

The **STAFFORDSHIRE BULL TERRIER** makes a wonderful family dog. He is splendid with children but can be tricky with other dogs unless under control. Whilst perhaps not built on the same elegant lines as some of the other breeds, his reliability with your family must recommend him to you. Finally there are the **DANDIE DINMONTS,** the **SKYES,** the **IRISH TERRIERS** and the **KERRY BLUES,** all worthy of consideration should your choice be a Terrier.

There then comes what is known as the working group. These breeds are defined as such as they are all guard dogs or working dogs. There are many among the 19 breeds which could interest you. It must be remembered

*Left, portrait of a Sheltie puppy aged five weeks.*
*Below, puppies are often difficult to identify when they are young – these are Saluki puppies aged five and a half weeks.*

that the guard dogs must have proper discipline and proper exercise. If you are able to take them to obedience classes (you will find these advertized in the dog papers or again the breeder can help you) this will be a great help in the forming of character and the occupying of their minds. This is most important in a guard dog. It is a fact that many of these are sold as pets and then either abandoned or returned to the breeders as being unmanageable when they are about a year, the main reason for this being because they were bored and shut up too much. Their active minds must be used, and they love to work in the same way as the gun dogs.

Though it may be argued these guard dogs, particularly the **ALSATIAN,** the **DOBERMAN** and the **ROTTWEILLER** have a greater intelligence than any other breed and ought to be strictly working dogs, the Alsatian makes a wonderful house dog given the right treatment in the right hands. He is adaptable, courageous and faithful and makes a

splendid guard dog. Every owner will tell you what a delightful pet he is. Unfortunately he was given a bad name because packs were originally used to hunt wolves and it has clung to him all these years. Many dogs bite people and the fact is never in the press, but if an Alsatian bites anybody it is at once headline news.

Only last year I saw one walking along the sea wall in St Ives with two small boys aged about seven and nine. They were alone, except for the dog who followed wherever they went. If one stopped, the dog stopped too, keeping an eye on the other one ahead. Sometimes they both went down on the sands and played about, whereupon their 'nannie' stopped with them. After watching for half an hour I discovered that this Alsatian was about ten years old, had been with the family all his life and was this morning on self-appointed guard duty.

There must be many stories that can be told of an Alsatian's devotion and bravery. If your choice falls on an

Alsatian, it is most important that you do buy one from a breeder, as in this way you can see the sire and the dam and probably its other relations as well. If you buy from a pet shop you will know nothing about its background.

**DOBERMANS** have also gained great popularity in recent years. They are shining black with tan, brown or blue markings. They stand 25 to 27 inches high and are smooth coated and most handsome. Full of fun and energy and great guard dogs, they require plenty of exercise and lots of human attention, though not spoiling, to exercise their minds as well as their bodies. They should not be kept in large numbers unless the owner is able to give individual time to the puppies when they are small. They are quick and intelligent, and will soon know how far they can go with you, so on no account spoil them. Above

all, exercise them.

Guard dogs come in all shapes and sizes. The two most formidable I have ever seen were on guard duty, also self appointed, in Trinidad. They were a cross of a Doberman and a Labrador and a Great Dane/Labrador. Their ears had been cropped as is done in the States with Danes and Dobermans. They were jet black with bright yellow piercing eyes, stood about 28 inches high and were exceedingly fierce-looking in every way. They took up their positions on either side of the drive gates, ears sharply pricked and every muscle taut. The young people of Trinidad always congregated outside these gates but they would never take one step inside them. Had they but known, the whole thing was a great big joke. These dogs, too, had a sense of humour and would have welcomed them with much snorting and snuff-

ling and barks of delight. They just pretended to look fierce and their whole appearance added to the illusion.

**ROTTWEILLERS** are also most reliable guards, but need careful training. Brought up strictly and taught obedience at an early age, they too could interest you.

The **BOXER** is the most popular of the smooth coated guard dogs. They too have a great sense of humour and your family will certainly enjoy this clown of a puppy. Their breed standard from the Kennel Club says that they are distrustful of strangers, but this does not appear to be so judging from their behaviour in the show ring as puppies. They are full of life and fun, so give your Boxer plenty of his own toys to play with or he will soon find something of yours. A very gay one swept his owner's dressing table clear one day and had a happy time

with all the cosmetics, finishing by swallowing her diamond ring. The vet suggested he was put on a rather stodgy diet and all exercise should be on a lead. It took all of three days before it finally appeared, much to everyone's relief. The puppy was none the worse.

Two others had high jinks with a small box of drawing pins. They discarded the box which gave the game away, but happily swallowed all the pins. A visit to the vet and use of an X-ray disclosed the pins in their stomachs, so they were fed a meal and then given a walnut-sized knob of washing soda. This made them sick so up came the meal and some of the drawing pins. The operation was repeated three or four times and finally all the pins were retrieved with no ill results. Luckily they were greedy puppies and were delighted to be given food at such frequent intervals.

These stories of foreign bodies being eaten by dogs brings to mind a Labrador which had eaten a leather driving glove. Given the soda treatment, he obligingly brought it up but before anyone could pick it up he had grabbed it and swallowed it again. This happened twice more before anyone was quick enough to get it

*A Beagle family playing together.*

from him. He thought it was a great game.

A Boxer is a dog which will give you great pleasure as he will settle down and forget his boisterous ways as he gets older. Being fine coated, his grooming will not take too much time. Colours are various although they are never all white.

The **GREAT DANE** is the tallest of the guard dogs, and is sometimes called the 'Gentle Giant'. He stands at least 28 to 30 inches at the shoulder and weighs in the region of 120 pounds, so his food bill will be a consideration as will the fact that he wants plenty of room for free exercise. They are disarmingly quiet dogs for their size once adult. The puppies have a charm all their own with their big knobbly knees and whilst certainly full of life, they are not quite so wild in their play as some of the other breeds mentioned. They love people and as a rule children too, but should not be bought for a very young family as they can frighten a small child without meaning to do so just in play alone. However, if you want a really big guard dog, here is a breed

with which you will also be happy.

The **BULL MASTIFF** and **ENGLISH MASTIFF** are both good guard and companion dogs, not requiring as much galloping as the other breeds. Neither are really children's dogs. The English Mastiff in particular takes himself rather seriously and whilst as a puppy he might enjoy a romp with a child, he would soon tire of the idea. Both are very handsome and very large, and the English in particular is a really massive dog.

The **SHEEPDOG BREEDS** are all lovely pets. The **ROUGH COLLIE** is the largest of them and most spectacular in looks. He has a beautiful coat which requires attention as often as possible. As a child's companion he has often been publicized by the artists. A Collie puppy is most attractive and when adult he will have great dignity of bearing. His head is especially attractive with his semi-erect ears and charming expression.

The **SHETLAND SHEEPDOG** is very like the Rough Collie only much smaller being only 14 inches high whereas the Collie is about 22 inches –

*Above, a basketful of long-haired Chihuahuas. These minute dogs stand only eight inches high.*
*Right, friends in spite of the incredible difference in size – an Irish Wolfhound and a Miniature Dachshund puppy.*

24 for the dogs. The little Sheltie is most appealing too, somewhat more retiring in character, it is very affectionate but takes a little longer to make friends. Never bad tempered, it has a certain reserve with strangers. He is very pretty in every way with the same sort of coat as the Collie which will require quite a lot of grooming and care. The result in both cases is well worth the trouble.

The **BEARDED COLLIE** is one that seems neglected as a pet, perhaps because it is not so often seen. It has the most delightful character and it would be well worth a visit to a kennel to see this breed. They have the most charming expressions and as small puppies would really attract you. They have shaggy coats with a fall of hair over their eyes and are lively bright companions somewhat

*Above, a Cavalier King Charles Spaniel.*
*Left, a four weeks old Wire-haired Dachshund puppy.*
*Right, a Great Dane puppy.*

smaller in height than Collies. Like them they are a working breed.

The **BOB TAIL SHEEPDOG** is another working dog but should be kept in the country, he is not a town dog. He is about 22 inches high and has a profuse dense coat with a handsome head covered with hair and shading his eyes. He has great bone and substance, and is a real character, but you must have space for him and be prepared to spend time on his coat.

**PYRENEAN MOUNTAIN DOG.** This breed is included here in detail owing to his great popularity in recent years. Unfortunately the breeders have had to start a Rescue Service, as so many people have bought puppies not realizing they would grow so big. There was a great demand for them, following one of the breed winning Best in Show at Crufts, a show which is known the world over. They are quite unsuitable for a flat or house with no garden. This is not only because of their height which is 27 to 32 inches, but also their girth and substance in body which runs from 36 to 42 inches. They are majestic and noble dogs,

*A Bull Terrier bitch with her puppies. These fun-loving, affectionate dogs have very strong characters and it was a Bull Terrier that was the champion dog at Cruft's in 1972.*

originating from France where they were used to guard the shepherd and his sheep. They also guarded the homes as they now do here. The wonder dog was Charles Zabronski of Pondtail who had all the attributes of the breed. In his lifetime he must have been a great advertisement for them. His bearing was extremely noble and the manner in which he accepted all the admiration he so justly deserved was just like that of a king. As indeed he was – a king among dogs.

They are all-white in colour, some with a few markings of badger-grey or varying shades of tan. As they have a dense undercoat with a long thick outer coat, they do need good grooming to keep it in order. However, they are well worth any trouble you have to spend on them. Like the puppies of all the dogs of this size, they must not be over indulged, obedience should be taught from the start of your ownership. They are extremely intelligent and quick to learn.

**ST BERNARDS** are in demand too, in spite of their size which is as great as that of the Pyranean, in fact their breed standard states 'the taller the better'. They also have dense thick coats which must be attended to frequently. They need careful rearing as do all the big breeds. This will be dealt with in the following chapter.

In colour they are very pleasing, being orange, mahogany brindle, or red brindle, with white patches on the body. They should have a white muzzle, white blaze up the face, white collar, white chest, white fore-legs, white feet and a white tip to the tail. They should have black shadings on the face and ears, with dark eyes, a black nose and a straight tail. It is quite possible to buy a puppy with in-correct points for a lower price than the show puppy. A litter is not often entirely perfect, and as the puppies are by no means cheap to rear the breeder would no doubt welcome you as a purchaser of a puppy for a pet.

**WELSH CORGIS, PEMBROKE**

**and CARDIGAN.** The former are certainly the most popular of the two varieties. They rose to fame through the Royal Family who have so many as their pets. They have maintained their status for a long time now, like the Cocker Spaniel, as so many owners continue with the same breed. They have an individuality all of their own. They are small, only 10 to 12 inches at the shoulder. Their little foxy faces and prick ears, coupled with their red coats and flashy white feet and chest markings certainly catch the eye. There are other mark-ings as well but these seem to be the most popular. The coat should be short and dense, but sometimes a

fluffy puppy appears in a litter, and the breeder would be willing to let you have this one at a reduced price, as they are not popular in the show ring. They are however very attractive in appearance and just as sweet as pets.

The **NORWEGIAN BUHUND** de-serves some mention as he makes an ideal house pet with a charming nature. The numbers imported have grown in recent years because of these attributes and also because of his small size, approximately 17 inches. He has a Spitz-type head with erect ears, dark eyes and a bright expres-sion. He has a close dense coat of various colours from wheaten through to wolf, sable, black and red. He has

a tight, curly tail and a strong compact body – in fact he might just be the one for you.

The **SAMOYED** – the all white sledge dog is one of the friendliest of the working breeds. His head and expression go to show this as his black lips seem to turn up at the corners giving him a 'smiling face'. They have a dense white, white and biscuit or cream coat, the outer tips of which should glisten in the sun when they are in full coat. They have a long tail carried over their backs, and their feet are unusual in that they are rather like moccasins, and hairy between the toes. This is an essential for them as they were primarily used for sledge work and still are in America for the Alaskan sledge races held there every year. The law does not allow dogs to be worked in that way in this country, but the 'Sammies' have not forgotten that this was one of their jobs in life.

The **SIBERIAN HUSKY** and the **ALSATIAN MALAMUTE** should be mentioned though there are only a few in this country. They are very popular in America where they are used for the sledge racing. Both are most handsome and exciting dogs to own. They are headstrong and require firm handling. They are tough, being used to extreme climates, and they like to live outdoors. The Husky is smaller and softer in coat than his more upstanding but equally noble-looking cousin the Malamute, which has distinctive head markings. Try and see these at a show, you will be impressed by them.

The Utility or Companion dog group should be headed by the **POODLES**, Standard, Miniature and Toy. These are the three sizes, the first being about 23 inches in height, while the Miniatures must not be over 15 inches or under 11 inches, and the little Toys

*Pet wire-haired Fox Terriers (above) and West Highland Whites (right) have a very great appeal.*

must be under 11 inches. The Toys are the most difficult to breed correctly and consequently the most expensive to purchase if you want one with any idea of showing it. At the present time this size is the most popular according to the Kennel Club registrations. The Miniature comes next with the Standard a long way behind, no doubt because of its size and the trouble of coping with its coat. It cannot be due to anything else, as he is a perfect pet. He is bold and at the same time affectionate. He has nobility as well as being a true sporting dog. In fact if you are able to have a larger dog, he combines all the qualities of many of the other breeds. There are plenty of dog pet parlours

which can cope with his coat for you if you can't manage it yourself. It does, however, require attention every eight to ten weeks and can therefore become somewhat costly.

The Miniatures were at one time the second most popular dog. In 1965 the Kennel Club registered no less than 11,377, the only breed to top them being the Alsatians with 12,572. But now they are down to 4,497 and the Alsatians have increased to 13,857. It is difficult to understand this drop in these lovely pets. Unfortunately popularity does not help a breed, in fact it does harm. Too many want to 'cash in' on the rise, too many bitches are indiscriminately mated and the first thing to suffer is temperament. There is no doubt that too many nervous and shy Miniatures have been bred. This is so sad, as they are the most intelligent, attractive, gay and long lived pets, and also have strong sporting instincts. My own poodle has been out shooting and one memorable day was allowed in a rabbit pen on a very famous trainer's estate. The gundogs were on check cords, she was being carried, but her eyes were nearly popping out of her head and her ears nearly meeting on top. The trainer seeing her intense excitement sat his pupils and said 'Let the wee lassie have a go.' – She went head over heels into the bushes after the rabbits, and though she did not catch one she nearly caught a pheasant by its tail and had the time of her life.

They must not be spoilt and given in to all the time, as they are very strong willed and you have to be firm with the Poodle puppy that persists in 'night calling', as they seem to be able to keep it up for longer than most breeds. It will be a battle of wills between you, and you must win at the start. If you establish your unquestioned authority you will then have a dog without equal. Remember the coat is the same as that of the Standard and must be trimmed within the same period of time. They can both be given what is known as the 'Lamb' cut, that is short all over the body with the legs left slightly long and a pom-pom on the head. The feet can be neatly rounded up and not clipped between the toes as in the show dog. Do not try using clippers

*Puppies of no particular breed that are just as attractive as the pedigrees.*

yourself until you are proficient at the job or you may produce a 'clipper' rash which can be very painful to the dog. The breeder might be persuaded to show you the art.

Finally we come to the Toy Poodle and there is little to add to what has been said about the larger sizes. It is equally intelligent, and their smaller size may well make it possible to carry out the axiom that 'two are better than one'. I once saw two little black Toys at Kennedy Airport, USA, running free amongst a milling crowd of people though following a

family close to heel. While the tickets and baggage were being attended to, this little pair were whizzing in and out of the luggage trolleys and being talked to by all the passengers. One jumped over the weighing scales and inspected the moving conveyor belt. They really were the prime interest in the Departure Hall and everybody turned to watch them.

Another popular dog in this group is the **DALMATIAN**, a clear, black and white or liver and white spotted dog. His popularity has also spiralled since the 60s. His spots should not

be larger than a large coin and should not merge together into patches. The coat should be a sparkling white and the spots very clear black or liver. The eyes are bright, intelligent, and dark in the black ones and amber or hazel in the livers. He stands from 24 to 32 inches, according to sex, with strong straight legs, a well-muscled deep body, and his movement should be free and active. He is a splendid companion if you ride, as he used to follow the carriages in the old days, and will thoroughly enjoy a good run across country.

**BULLDOGS** enjoy a certain amount of popularity and their breeders will tell you what good house dogs they are. Known as the emblem of British dogs, their appearance is familiar to all. Some years ago there was a well-known bookmaker who owned a famous show Bulldog, called 'Queenie'. She did a lot to popularize the breed as her owner believed in advertising, so when she was being shown at any big outdoor show, he would hire an aeroplane to fly over the ground bearing a banner with her name and the slogan – 'Jimmy Knode, Always wears a rose; and never owes' to help his business.

The **BOSTON TERRIER** is another smooth-coated dog, and is brindle-coloured with very distinctive white markings. They vary in size and weight and can be up to 20 to 25 pounds. The smaller ones seem to be the most popular. They are sharp and intelligent with small erect ears and are neat and easy to have in the house with their short sleek coats.

**FRENCH BULLDOGS** are not unlike the Boston in appearance to the casual observer, though of course a

breeder will look for different points. They too have erect ears and a short nose and tail; but they are somewhat bigger than the Boston and are not as quick and active. However, their owners love them for their faithful natures.

**CHOW CHOWS** are very popular, and have been increasing in numbers since 1965. A show puppy is certainly an eye catcher. However as an adult they are serious by nature and not as outgoing as many of the other breeds. They would not welcome too much attention from a band of teenagers fussing over them all at once. Consequently, whilst ideal for a small family, they would not fit in as well with several children. There may always be exceptions to the rule, but in this case it would be essential to buy a puppy and not an adult. They are most handsome dogs, growing up to be about 18 inches high. They are whole coloured black, red, fawn, blue, cream or white, though it is unusual to see the latter colour in the show ring. Their heads are most lion-like and very attractive with the small, erect ears which show the characteristic 'scowl' when they are pricked forward. They have compact strong bodies, with the tail carried well over the back, and a very big coat which looks most handsome when it is full.

The **KEESHOND** is not unlike the Chow in body and general type but has a foxy head and small erect ears. He has a most attractive expression as his dark eyes are surrounded by 'spectacles', which is the term for the dark shading of the coat round them. His height is about 17 to 18 inches; he is compact in body with a tail curled tightly over his back. He is a most charming and intelligent dog, very gay and active. His wolf or ash-grey coat is dense and off-standing and he has cream-coloured legs and a plume to his tail with a black tip which

*Above, a Rough Collie with her five baby puppies.*
*Top right, Italian Greyhound bitch with her two puppies.*
*Below right, Great Dane pups, black, blue, fawn, harlequin and brindle.*

makes him a most good-looking animal. The puppies of course have great appeal. They originated from Holland, where they were guard dogs on the barges.

In this group also comes the **SCHIPPERKE**, a smooth-coated black or cream little dog originally used to give warning of strangers on the Belgian barges. They are good guard dogs, neat and very intelligent, weighing only about 12 to 16 pounds. They have bright foxy faces and most expressive bright eyes. Their erect ears and alert manner, smooth coat and thick mane round their necks make them a very smart house dog.

The last of this family are the

**SCHNAUZERS** who come in three sizes, 'Giant' of which there are not many in this country, 'Medium' and the 'Miniature' all of which have the same points. It is the Miniature which is the most popular and very smart he is too. Only 13 to 14 inches high, he has a square body and well proportioned head with lovely eyes, neatly covered with bushy eyebrows. He is pepper and salt or black in colour, and his coat must be trimmed for show, or even as a house pet as you would enjoy his extra smart appearance. He has a very extrovert and sparkling personality and makes an excellent pet.

Taking the group of hound breeds to include 21 breeds, there are a great many among them you will want to see before making your final choice. As there are six varieties of **DACHS-HUNDS** these will head the list, starting with the Smooth-haired Miniatures. These have the most registrations with the Long-Haired Miniatures close behind. As a pet dog one seems to see more standard Smooth-haired dogs around, while the two Wire-haired varieties are not nearly so popular. The 'Mins' are probably so popular owing to their size, which is very handy indeed for the house. They are full of vim and vigour, and love going for walks. They make

*Left, Standard Poodles and their puppies.*
*Right and below, a family of Miniature Poodles. These dogs only stand about 20 inches high.*

excellent children's pets and companions, as they are easy to look after and handle. It is better to have the standard size for this purpose, as they can be used for hunting and digging at which they excel. They are very teachable and intelligent and most faithful to their owners.

One quite old one had an adventure during the war which proved both these points. She lived with her mistress who was in the ATS in one district whilst her master, also in the army, was stationed some distance away. She spent some time with each of them. On one particular occasion they met in a strange town near a park, where they left their cars. On parting to return to their respective billets, each thought the other had taken the dog. It was not until the next day when talking on the telephone was it discovered that neither had her. Of course panic ensued and each dashed off to the park. There she was patiently still sitting on the seat where they had left her.

The **WHIPPETS** are another breed that can charm you, both for size and intelligence and the ease with which they can be kept. You can also have a lot of fun with them among the Amateur Racing owners. There are several Clubs in existence now which cater for the pet owner as well as the show owner. The breeder can give you all the necessary details, should your choice be the 'Miners' dog' as it used to be called. In the old days many of the miners in the north of England owned them for racing only, and mighty were the wagers laid on them. Woe betide you if you in your fancy motor car ran one down, better you ran over his child than his whippet.

In those days they raced to a flag waved by the owner from one end of a long field. Held by his friend at the opposite end, when the whistle blew the dog would be literally hurtled forward; this was most skilfully done and an expert thrower could gain yards for the dog. Now they race from traps like the greyhounds but they love it just the same. Their appearance being well-known, it is unnecessary to describe it here, and if you

*Left, the elegant head of a young Whippet dog.*
*Right, hardly necessary . . . unless to beware of falling for him.*

want to race do not buy a big one as they are not as good. This is a breed that must have warmth and in cold weather should be kept 'rugged up.' Dog coats especially suitable for whippets can be purchased at most pet shops. This is very essential.

**GREYHOUNDS.** These are the 'Cinderellas' of the dog world. They may appear to lack character or affection and to have a tendency to go for other dogs or kill your cat, but when you get to know them you will realize that nothing could be further from the truth. Those that are given away from the racing kennels have, of course, been taught to chase anything that runs. The only life they have known is chasing a mechanical hare round a race track, consequently they are always on the look-out for movement, even a leaf or a piece of paper will attract their attention. This is natural and understandable, but they are still good pets.

The show Greyhound is quite different, and a puppy has all the charm and affection of any other breed. He loves to play and when older will hunt any game he finds. As I have bred many for show and as pets I can vouch for their integrity. They also love children, and one dog I knew used to go off every day through the woods to the village school playground, arriving just in time for the children's playtime. The children loved him and he loved them and joined in all their games. When the holidays came and there were no cries to greet him, he gave it up after three or four visits but to keep him happy he was sold to a family with children and lived to a good old age.

Therefore if you would like a greyhound as your first pet do not listen to the horror stories about them. Go to a breeder and get a puppy, as they will give you endless pleasure in every way.

**BEAGLES** are another breed which many people have as pets both in town and country. They are hounds and love to hunt and have free access to fields where they can gallop as they should. Like most of the 'pack' breeds, they can be deaf to all commands when they choose. It is there-

*Two Yorkshire Terrier puppies. These are the most popular of the toy dogs, and have long silky coats which hang down from a parting on either side of their backs unless they are trimmed.*

fore important you teach them strict obedience when they are small, for this reason have a puppy. Their popularity arises certainly from the fact they are small, 16 inches at the highest. They are short coated so do not trail mud in the house, and a minimum of grooming is required. In common with all the hound breeds they are affectionate and intelligent.

The same can be said of the **BASSET**, who is the clown among the hounds. As a house pet he can give you great amusement. He really does seem to play to the gallery. For instance he loves to do 'trampoline' on the sofa cushions – up and down, getting higher and higher, until finally he gets it right for the final plunge. He always casts a quick look round to see if he is getting attention. He is a very loving and faithful companion, but he must have exercise, for if not, he will go out and find it for himself. He likes the companionship of other dogs, so think about having two instead of one of this breed also.

**AFGHANS** are a most exotic breed and one which will be admired by all your friends. As baby puppies they have great charm with their whiskery faces. They have suddenly gained tremendous popularity, so do be certain you buy a puppy with really good temperament and see his parents at the time of purchase. They are tall dogs, anything from 25 to 29 inches. They have beautiful flowing long coats, which get matted very easily if you do not attend to them regularly. They must have plenty of freedom as they are full of life and fun, especially when puppies. As they grow older, they develop a more aloof attitude towards strangers but they will be devoted to you and your family.

The **SALUKI** comes into the same category though he is much smaller, and having a short-haired coat he is easier to care for. They are more lightly made, very beautiful and graceful in build, they are also charming and faithful in character. They

*Top left, the French Bulldog is very different from the English and is also much smaller. He makes a delightful pet though he must not be allowed to get too fat.*
*Left and right, Bulldogs may not be the most beautiful of creatures but they have very gentle and affectionate natures.*

love to gallop, in fact they almost fly when they go fast. They have the most beautiful eyes and expression. Like the smaller Eastern breeds, they are very regal and dignified and should not be made fun of. A Saluki as a household companion is very desirable.

The **IRISH WOLFHOUND** is another 'gentle giant' which you should not consider as a house pet unless you are able to give him the space and freedom he should have. The largest of the hounds, 28 to 34 inches being the desired height, he loves to be free as he is a running dog. Given the right environment he is a grand friend and companion. He has an even temperament, and is affectionate without being 'sloppy'. He is a most handsome dog with a rough, harsh coat, which is short and not too much worry to groom. His colour is generally grey, or brindle, red, black, pure white and fawn. The Irish Guards have one as a mascot and very imposing he looks on parade; he takes his duties as seriously as his position befits.

The **DEERHOUND** is almost his counterpart, though much more lightly made, as he is built for great speed and used for coursing. Though nearly the same height, he has not the same great substance in body. In colours there is little difference, except that all-white is not recognized in this hound. He has the most lovely head with a very sweet soft expression, enhanced by his dark eye rims, and small mouse-like ears. He is graceful in outline, rather like a greyhound, whilst his character, sweet nature and poise is all you could wish for in your pet. In the event of your being able to keep a large hound, it will not be an easy choice for you to make.

The **BLOODHOUND** is a great hound and yet another which will intrigue you, though here again he must have space. There are many, however, that do not live with all the country facilities they should have as they are used for showing rather than for working. However, they are very dignified and seem to accept their

*Left, a Great Dane puppy waiting to be let in.*
*Top right, two King Charles Spaniel puppies.*
*Right, a family of American Cocker Spaniels.*
*Following page: Golden Cocker Spaniels.*

*Above, every puppy is attractive . . .*
*Far left, a Labrador puppy.*
*Top left, a Basset Hound and her large family.*
*Left, two young Salukis.*

position in life in a philosophical manner. They measure about 23 to 26 inches with great substance in body and heavy in bone. They have a most fascinating head with long pendulous ears and loose skin which falls into wrinkles on either side when their heads are held down to scent. They are very handsome dogs, affectionate companions and very sensitive to correction though not nervous. In fact most hounds are more sensitive to your voice than other breeds, except perhaps the Toys.

Bloodhounds are known for their extraordinary scenting powers. For some reason they are not made so much use of here except for the Hound Trials. These you must see as a Bloodhound owner. In America, however, they are used to track missing persons and one performed a wonderful feat in finding a missing child. This hound was kennelled with a private owner but made available to the police at any time. A little boy was lost; he had last been seen in a crowded hardware store on the outskirts of a busy village, bounded by

woods at one end, and had been missing for 24 hours. The Bloodhound was called in and given the child's pyjamas and some things he had handled in the shop to smell. Everyone stood back in anticipation waiting to see the dog's reaction. He nosed around in the shop, then went out of the door, scented around and finally set off down the road towards the woods. He hesitated a few times, but finally entered the wood and went along a small track through the trees. He halted at the end by a large hole and there at the bottom was the small boy none the worse for his adventure. He had obviously climbed down and then was unable to get out again, and but for the Hound, would probably never have been found.

**BORZOIS.** These Russian hounds are among the aristocrats of the hound breeds; they too are quite tall and can be 27 to 29 inches tall. They do look very aristocratic as they have long fine heads, and are rather greyhound-like in shape and body, with long tails which are nicely plumed with silky hair. Their body coat is shorter and they move with a very light, free action. In their own land they were used for hunting wolves but that was long ago, and now they are the most decorative of house dogs and can have a very warm affection for their owners.

The **ELKHOUND** is one of the smaller hounds, very popular with his breeders and a smart, keen, happy dog. His height is 18 to 20 inches. He has pricked ears, with bright dark eyes. His compact sturdy body is covered with a dense coarse coat and he carries his curled tail over his back. They are of Nordic origin and are keen hunting dogs given the opportunity. They are very friendly too, not only towards you but your friends as well.

The two smaller Hounds are the **FINNISH SPITZ** and the **BASENJI.** The Finkie, as the breeders refer to him, makes an excellent pet. He is attractive in looks with a sharp foxy face, erect ears and dark eyes. This can make you give him a second look as he also has a black nose, and a bright red coat with lighter shadings on his tail. Altogether he is a very showy, well-balanced and smart dog. In Finland where he originated he is used to mark game birds in the woods. He has excellent eye sight and sees the birds in the trees, runs along as they fly and watches where they land. He then stands sentinel below and barks with a rather loud high bark to tell his master where they are. He makes a very good house dog, being small, 16 to 17 inches, and though he has an off-standing dense coat, he keeps himself extremely clean.

The Basenji is known as the Bark-

73

less dog, though he makes up for this with a kind of yodel or deep whine in his throat. He is another breed which is very clean and easy to keep in the house. He has a very pretty head with pricked ears and he wrinkles his forehead when interested, which enhances his expression. He has a short coat of bright red, or all-black, and black and tan. He has white feet and chest and a white tip to his tail. This is curled lightly over his back. The puppies are most attractive as their wrinkles are more obvious. They only came here in 1934 and were found in Africa. They are a most unusual breed with a very distinctive and charming character, quiet and undemanding in the house, yet willing and eager to join in the family fun.

The Toy group covers 15 breeds of which the **PEKINESE** is the most popular as a pet. If you have decided you want a Toy breed, this is probably the one you will go to see first, but have a look at the others before finally deciding. A Peke puppy is certainly most engaging. They are very friendly, very gay and will certainly tug at your heart strings. Their appearance is known to most people. The Standard demands a flat face and a broad short nose with large open nostrils. It is important you see that he does have these latter points. Unfortunately many have tiny little noses and small nostrils which are deeply imbedded in their faces. This should be avoided as it can affect their breathing as they grow older. They are very intelligent and extremely bossy so do not let them have all their own way or you will become their slaves.

The **GRIFFON BRUXELLOIS** and the **GRIFFON BRABANÇON** – The former are rough coated and the latter are smooth. They are such clever little dogs that it is surprising they are not so popular as the Pekinese. They have little monkey-like turned up faces with lovely expressive eyes, little short cobby bodies and semi-erect ears. Their colours are bright clear red, black, or black with a nice bright tan.

All their owners will tell you that they are most responsive, in fact they seem to have the gift of anticipation. This certainly seems to be true judging by the stories about them. They are very brave for their small size and nothing daunts them. I heard of one who ran round the corner of a country lane and was faced with a pack of hounds out at summer exercise. They all advanced towards him, while the owner and the huntsman stood rooted to the spot, feeling sure this would be his end. He was quite unperturbed and stood his ground, letting the pack circle him which they did for several

*Right, a Poodle puppy.*
*Below, a Smooth-haired Miniature Dachshund and a Pug sharing the hearth rug with a kitten.*

nerve-wracking moments. Finally they all went on their way, and the huntsman in passing, said in thankful tones, 'What a brave little dog. If he had run they would have torn him to pieces.'

The **CHIHUAHUA**, smooth coat and long coat. You may want a very small dog, if so these are the smallest of the Toys. They weigh up to 6 pounds and very often much less. They have a round apple-shaped head with big ears which are erect, set

out at an angle. They have very expressive full eyes and have a very cheeky expression when alert, which they are most of the time. They become attached to their owners and their home and, like the Griffon, will guard it against all comers. As they are so small the stranger does not usually realize he is being attacked. They cling to a man's trousers, shaking them vigorously and screaming with fury. The visitor generally laughs saying what funny little dogs they

are. They certainly give good warning with their acute hearing, and nobody would get into your house without them telling you. Despite their small size they are very strong and healthy and highly prized by the breeders.

The **CAVALIER KING CHARLES SPANIEL** is yet another of the Toys which has achieved great popularity. He is a gay, active and very sporting breed. He has a longish, flat, silky coat of several colours: black and tan,

ruby, which is a rich red, and Blenheim, which is a bright chestnut broken up with the whitest of white. The latter should have a little spot or 'lozenge' of chestnut in the middle of his white head. There are also tricolours which have a black, white, and tan coat, so you have a good variety to choose from. They generally have very good and even temperaments, and are not prone to shyness. A Cavalier is a glamorous dog and a pet well worthy of your consideration.

The **KING CHARLES SPANIEL** has been seen in many of the portraits from the Old Masters, but as yet has not gained the popularity of the Cavalier. He has a most distinctive head, well domed with very lovely and expressive eyes. He weighs 8–14 pounds, so is very suitable for a small apartment.

The **ENGLISH TOY TERRIER** is very Terrier-like in his outlook on life though he is a Toy. In his early days before dog shows were the rage, he

*Welsh Springer Spaniels showing their sturdy build and strong legs, which they need when retrieving game all day in rough country.*

was used in 'Rat Pits' and used to kill an astonishing number of rats in a short space of time, in spite of his diminutive size – he only weighs 6 to 8 pounds and stands 10 to 12 inches at the shoulder. His bright dark eyes are full of expression and his long narrow head is set up by erect ears. He has a fine shining black coat with tan points, and he is neat and cleanly built, and therefore ideal for you in a small place.

This also applies to the **JAPANESE SPANIEL**, which weighs only 7 pounds. They are fine boned with plenty of long coat which can be black and white, red and white, and other shades of sable, brindle, lemon and orange. They have a very pretty head with small ears, carried slightly forward. Their ears are large and dark and they should show white in the inner corners, which gives them a surprised expression possessed by no

other breeds, sometimes referred to as a 'squint', which is quite inaccurate. They are very charming little dogs and the puppies are quite delightful.

The **PAPILLON** or Butterfly dog as he is sometimes called is yet another charmer. The name is given him because of his large ears which he holds out at an angle when he grows up. They are fringed with hair at the sides and do give the idea of a butterfly's wings, especially when they are held erect. Some have a fully dropped ear which is also correct. Like the Japanese, they are small and dainty with a happy and lively personality. They also have a flowing coat but it is easy to manage as it has no undercoat.

The **POMERANIAN** is a lovely Toy Breed, and in full coat one which will also tempt you very much, and so will the puppies as they are quite enchanting. When adult they are from $4\frac{1}{2}$

*A healthy, intelligent and happy Dalmatian puppy playing in the spring sunshine. He is just ten weeks old and his spots are well developed – they do not appear until the puppies are two to three months old.*

pounds. They have the sweetest little foxy faces with small erect ears, and there is a fascinating range of colours. They are very intelligent and bright, and fun to own. Their profuse coat will need care.

The **MALTESE** is another fully-coated Toy whose silky flowing coat nearly touches the ground. It is, however, fairly easy to manage as it has no woolly undercoat. It is pure white in colour and the whole dog is most appealing with its dark eyes and eye rims and black nose. It is 10 inches high and very suitable if your home is in the town. It has a very happy

nature and moves with great speed for such a small dog.

**PUGS**, and in particular Pug puppies are enchanting creatures with large round heads, black masks and small dark ears. They have square sturdy bodies, smooth glossy coats and weigh 14 to 18 pounds. They have very jolly characters and their large dark eyes are most attractive.

**YORKSHIRE TERRIERS.** Though these dogs have long silky coats which hang down from a parting down the centre of their backs, they are by no means soft in character. In fact, they have a very Terrier-like expression. Their heads are bright tan in colour with erect or semi-erect ears, whilst the body coat, though black when they are puppies, should turn a nice dark steel blue. They are sharp bouncy little puppies and though the show breeders encourage the length of coat, you, as the pet owner, can keep it short. As a character the 'Yorkie' is an excellent companion.

The **MINIATURE PINSCHER** is one of the smartest of the Toys and a 'Min Pin' puppy can give you a lot of pleasure as he is a very sparkling little dog. He is 10 to 12 inches high, and has a smooth coat of black, blue or chocolate with tan markings. He has a fascinating 'hackney' action and is quite fearless and very self-possessed at all times, given the right training.

The **ITALIAN GREYHOUND** is another Toy whose picture has been seen many times in the Old Masters. A Greyhound in miniature, he is very fine boned with a fine skin and a coat just like satin. Whilst they are full of life and fun, they are not a breed for a large family. They feel the cold and love to curl up under the blankets on your bed. They would not appreciate being out in the rain and the wind, though they love their walks the same as any other dog. They are not delicate but they need care as they only weigh 6 to 8 pounds. You would have a most loving and sweet little dog if you buy an 'I.G.' as they are sometimes called.

**SHIH TZUS** and **LHASA APSOS** are both Tibetan breeds and used for guarding the temples in their native

*Top, smooth-coated Fox Terriers are one of the most attractive of the Terrier breeds and are lively, courageous and hardy.*
*Left, a wire-haired Fox Terrier.*
*Right, a Jack Russell Terrier.*

*Above, two tiny Pembrokeshire Corgis.*
*These dogs have their tails docked.*
*They make excellent house pets.*
*Left, a Golden Retriever family.*

land. The former are now greatly in demand and their registrations have shot up from 499 in 1965 to 1,453 in 1971, and have also been registered in America. They have won their way into the hearts of their owners, and the general public are intrigued by them because of their quaint appearance – sometimes it is difficult to tell the back from the front owing to their long coats. Their characters and general attitude to their owners is quite unlike those of most other breeds. They are most independent, yet loving and affectionate, and they have tremendous dignity. You must never order them about but rather ask politely 'Please will you come here' or 'Would you mind getting off that chair please.' They are very active and extremely agile for their

size, which is between 9 and 16 pounds. They hold themselves with pride with their tails curled over their backs. They have a round head with beautifully expressive eyes hidden by a shock of hair, which can be tied up with a rubber band or ribbon. The hair grows upwards over the noses which is how they have been sometimes called 'chrysanthemum' dogs. They have a jaunty and distinctive action, flipping their back legs out behind as they go along generally at a great pace. They love to sit up high on the back of a chair or a sofa, or on a wide window seat, this is perhaps a relic of their temple days when they wanted to see who was coming – friend or foe.

They come in a variety of shades, which are very attractive but in all of them a white blaze on the forehead and a white tip to the tail, as the Standard quotes, are highly prized. The long coat can be a problem if you do not look after it, but they have such individuality and charm it is well worth the extra trouble; surely any

pet is worth trouble for the pleasure it brings.

The Lhasa Apso or Tibetan Apso as they are also called, has much the same look and characteristics. They are somewhat bigger and longer in face and perhaps when adult are more reserved than the Shih Tzus. The best colour for them is golden or the lion-like colours, and they are sometimes referred to as the Tibetan Lion dog.

A cousin of the Lhasa Apso is the **TIBETAN TERRIER**, a somewhat shaggy dog not unlike a small Bob Tail Sheepdog. He was also used as a guard dog, but outside the temples, whereas the others were inside. He is about 15 inches high with a very shaggy coat to keep him warm.

A study of the breed characteristics and size will perhaps have helped you to make your choice, but it is not easy – all young animals, and puppies in particular, are very attractive and endearing.

# Rearing and training a puppy

*Two Norfolk Terriers. These puppies are identical to the Norwich Terriers except that their soft ears are dropped while those of the Norwich are erect; no distinction is recognized in America. These are true Terriers, fun-loving, affectionate and sturdy.*

When setting out to buy your puppy you should take with you a small rug in which to wrap him, and if you are going to have him on your knee, have a towel and small bowl. Sometimes a first car ride will cause a puppy to be sick and it is easiest to push a container under his chin when he starts to 'heave'. You may not get any warning, so be prepared and spread the towel over your knees. As previously stated, small puppies generally travel well but do try and take him about with you from the first. You may prefer to take a box with you for the first journey, but if he is of a size to sit on your lap, he will be comforted and consequently not be frightened by his first experience.

When you get home, do not let everyone crowd round nor invite your neighbours in to see him. If he is small, like the baby too much excitement could upset him. Explain to your children he is like a new boy at school, everything is strange and you must give him time to get acclimatized. Do not be disappointed if the bold gay puppy you collected at the kennel is suddenly overcome by all the strange sights and noises of his new home, and goes all shy. A few soothing words and a small meal will soon bring him round again. One of the best ways to reassure him is to sit down on the floor and let him come to you. If he has disappeared under a chair, do *not* try to drag him out as this will only scare him. Have patience and let him come out by himself, and use your voice a lot. So many owners do not talk to their dogs, and a small puppy will get great comfort from you if you encourage him in this way.

The best bed for a puppy of the small breeds is a small wooden box turned on its side, with a small piece of wood tacked across the front to keep his cushion or blanket from falling out. This is much more comforting than the open basket which most people tend to buy. It is also useful in training him to stay at home alone, as it can be turned with the opening at the top so that his blanket or bed is at the bottom, and he cannot then get out unaided. Give him a hot water bottle wrapped in a bag or a piece of blanket. This will help to console him for the loss of his brothers and sisters. Of course he will protest at first and some will take longer than others to accept being alone. Do not be tempted to lift him out. You may decide he is to sleep in your bedroom, in which case still stick to the box routine. If you think he wants to go out to attend to the calls of nature, take him out and if he obliges be sure to praise him. In this way the basis of his house training will be laid. Of course no small puppy can go right through the night without making a puddle. Therefore if he cries in the night, have some newspaper laid down near his box and encourage him to use it. Many flat owners who have pets train their dogs in this way. However, if you have a garden try and train him to go outside as soon as possible.

It is most important that you put him out frequently – always first thing in the morning and last thing at night, *always* after food, and if he has been asleep during the day, whip him out as soon as he wakes up. It is better to prevent him making his 'mistakes' rather than correcting him afterwards. Try to arrange his arrival when you yourself are free to devote some time to him each day. He will have to learn to stay alone sometimes, so start off with short periods at first; if he barks, go back to him, saying 'No' in a firm tone and put him in his bed. Give him some toys such as the hard rubber bones sold at the pet stores, rather than anything soft that he can chew to pieces. His teeth can be very sharp and bits of rubber are certainly not good for him.

These stores also sell Beef Chewy sticks, which are excellent toys, and it does not matter if he eats them up in time. They are made of cow hide and cannot hurt him, what is more they will keep him happy and help his teething. The bigger breeds can soon make short work of them, so a large marrow bone can replace these. Be sure it is a marrow bone and not the kind that can splinter; examine it well to ensure there are no sharp pieces which are loose that he can swallow. Many owners give their puppies bones with no dire results and they are lulled into a false security thinking 'Bones don't hurt my puppy.' Then one day one gets stuck and the result can be fatal, or at best there has to be an operation to remove it, so be warned and do not chance it.

While on the subject of foreign bodies, puppies are very prone to pick up and swallow stones, coal etc., so if your puppy does eat something, remember the story of the ring and the drawing pins, and on no account give him castor oil. Always keep in the house a bottle of liquid paraffin. This is a soothing lubricant. One or

*Above, a Staffordshire Bull Terrier and her puppy.*
*Left, this Labrador puppy is out on an early training session, as an experienced and intelligent bitch is the best possible teacher when the puppies are still young.*

two teaspoons of this, according to the age and size of the puppy, will soothe his inside and help him to pass whatever he has swallowed. It can be put on his food as it is quite tasteless and he should not object to it.

If your puppy has not been inoculated, this is the first thing you must have done. The breeder can arrange this for you before purchase if you wish, which would be ideal. However, just in case this has not been possible a few words of advice may be judicious. On no account let him come in contact with any other dogs until after this has been done. Keep

him in your garden, in any case he only requires to scamper about and play in his early days. If you have a large breed puppy you can always play games with him to encourage him to take more exercise than the small breed puppy requires.

This inoculation is absolutely essential. *Do not* put off having it done – you may bring disease in to him on your shoes or clothes from other animals. He has a certain immunity from his mother against all diseases, but this only lasts up to about six to seven weeks, from that time he is extremely vulnerable, and small puppies have very little resistance.

Your vet can explain that the vaccination will protect him against all the four diseases which any puppy is prone to. Briefly these are Distemper or Hard Pad, Virus Hepatitis, which is a killer and can be effective in a very short time; Leptospirosis Cani-

cola, which attacks dogs living in towns and is also a killer, and finally an equally virulent one Leptospirosis Icterohaemorrhagiae, which is carried by rats which the country dogs come in contact with.

Dog owners are very fortunate that the scientists have developed these inoculations as a protection for their dogs. Before the war there were no such injections and breeders very often lost their whole stock if an attack of Distemper struck their kennels. It only requires two injections to protect him against all four of these dread diseases, *Do not delay, do it today.*

This should also be your slogan throughout your puppy's whole life. If at any time he shows any sign of illness, or refuses his food for more than a day do not force food on him. A cold nose is not always an indication of good health. If he seems dull

or out of sorts, 'phone your vet. He will not blame you if it is only a passing ailment, as he would much rather see a puppy at the very start of its illness and so have a better chance of a cure, than be faced with one already seriously ill. Baby puppies can go down hill very quickly.

If you want to be really helpful, buy an animal thermometer. These have a blunt end for the quicksilver unlike the human one. It is quite easy to take a puppy's temperature, which should be $101\frac{1}{2}°$ to $102°$, anything over this can indicate something not quite right. Do not take it after food or exercise. Stand the puppy on a table with somebody to support his tummy to keep him upright and also to re-assure him. Gently lift his tail up slightly, do not yank it up high and having well greased the end of the thermometer, insert it gently at a slightly upward angle in the rectum for a distance of about two inches, it should go in quite easily but if not the puppy may whip round, so your assistant should be prepared for this.

*Above, Old English Sheepdog puppies are really cuddly and playful but should only go to homes in the country.*
*Right, a Border Collie.*

Take it out and start again. However, should the puppy get frightened, do not persist as his very fright may cause the temperature to rise. If you succeed and find it is normal, it will set your mind at rest. On the other hand if it is up, say to $103°$ or over, then you should certainly 'phone your friend the vet.

When you buy your puppy make sure he has been wormed. This very necessary dosing should have been attended to at least once or twice before you had him; most puppies do have these pests but they are easily cured. Your vet will give you some pills that cause no discomfort and which are far safer and cost no more than the ones advertised by the pet stores.

You may see them in his motions, round worms are white and about

three inches long. Later on he can get what is known as tape worm, and there are pills for both kinds. An indication that your puppy may have worms is that his tummy will get very distended after his food, and his coat may also lose its shine. Anyway it does no harm to dose him, so ask your vet for some tablets to have by you.

*Fresh water should always be available for your puppy. Always* leave him a bowl down in the same place all day and every day from the moment you have him.

While on the subject of your puppy's care and before passing on to the important subject of feeding, he does not require collar and lead exercise before the age of four months but you can get him used to them both walking round your garden. Do not use a harness. Let him get used to a small rounded collar first of all, then attach the lead and let him trail it along. Finally pick it up and try and go with him so that he does not feel the pull of it. When he does he will probably plunge about but by having patience and giving a short lesson every day he will soon learn it does not hurt and by the time he is ready for walks he will be used to it.

**COAT CARE.** Any puppy should be groomed from the first to get him used to being handled and standing still and doing as he is told. Grooming is as good a way of teaching him as any. Unless he is one of the very large breeds, stand him on a table, making sure it is not a slippery surface and does not wobble about. Place your hand gently on his hindquarters and the other on his head, at the same time saying his name and the command 'sit'. Then proceed to brush and comb him.

A bristle or nylon and bristle brush is as good as any for all puppies

*Beagles under five weeks old dozing after their mid-day meal.*

except perhaps the very fine smooth coated ones, when a softer kind may be used. If he tries to jump down as he very well may, try and stop him and still in a quiet voice repeat the command. Try and say it in a bright way with a lift to the tone of voice when you sit 'sit'. When you want to groom his hindquarters and body you will want him standing up, so raise him to a standing position by putting your hand underneath his tummy and give him the command to stand, keeping your hand in position to prevent him sitting down again. Finally when you want him lying

down to groom his chest and tummy tell him to lie down. Many puppies do not like this and it will take time and patience before he will lie quietly. Make a fuss of him but try and keep him lying on his side. Only continue for a very short time each day – he will soon learn – never get impatient and never reward him with titbits, only praise after each part is finished.

If you can get him relaxed and at ease in his puppyhood, the business of grooming him when he has grown his full coat will be halved, and what is more you will have an obedient and happy dog. The puppies who get no

training of this kind are a misery to themselves and a menace when they go to the pet shop for trimming. There are some who are so naughty that their owners cannot groom them and their coats become matted to a degree when the vet has to come and give them a sedative before they can be touched. This is all the fault of the owner not being firm at first and not the fault of the dog.

When grooming keep a watchful eye that he has not picked up any livestock – this can happen in the best regulated household. They can pick up fleas or lice from the grass and of

course from other dogs. Should he get these pests you can either get a shampoo from your vet or the pet stores have various remedies you can brush into his coat.

**EARS.** It is also a good idea to get a small piece of surgical lint, wrap it round your finger, dip it in a weak solution of Peroxide of Hydrogen, and wipe it round inside his ears to keep them sweet and clean.

**TEETH.** These should be watched carefully especially in the Toy breeds, which do not shed them as easily as the larger breeds. Give them hard biscuits such as charcoal ones to chew to help their dentation; using the same kind of lint wrapped round your finger, dip it in a solution of a teaspoon of salt to one pint of water and clean all round the gums. It will help to prevent tartar forming on them. This forms very easily and if it gets bad as the dog grows older, do let your vet remove it for you. It is the cause of gum deterioration and bad breath too. This particularly applies to the smaller breeds.

**EYES.** Your puppy's eyes should not require much attention if he is in good health. Sometimes they do become a little runny, especially at the teething time; in which case just wipe them dry with a piece of cotton wool moistened but not too wet, in a weak solution of Boracic Lotion. Then dry them well. This can be done twice or three times a day. Never buy a puppy with running eyes – he may have been in a cold wind, but on the other hand he may have the start of Entropian or ingrowing eyelashes, which will require an operation to cure. Chows in particular are prone to this painful complaint. Unfortunately while the puppy is very small it is not apparent, as the lashes are very soft. He may not show any signs of this incipient trouble until he is about nine to ten weeks old. Chows are not the only breed which can develop this, so be sure and have a good look at the puppy's eyes on purchase. It is possible for any puppy to get a cold in the eyes. The consequent discharge can become crusted and sore – follow

*Above, a cross-bred puppy with an intelligent air.*
*Right, a pedigree Great Dane puppy aged three and a half months.*

the above procedure and then put a couple of drops of castor oil in them, or even wipe round the eyelids with the oil to keep them from getting dry. Gun dogs sometimes get eye injuries when hunting and the castor oil is good for these too.

In the case of a real eye injury do not go in for home treatment, go to your vet. During play Peke puppies sometimes get an eye right out. This is very alarming and requires immediate treatment. If your vet is not readily available, try and press it back yourself, lubricate it well with castor oil and lifting the eyelids up press it firmly back into the socket.

Of course, a vet is best, but if not attended to the eye cannot be saved. This does not often happen but it is by no means rare.

There is one other disease or condition about which a great deal is written and that is Progressive Retinal Atrophy. This is considered to be hereditary. Many kennel owners have their breeding stock tested for it as there are several breeds afflicted. It is a form of night blindness that shows itself gradually. The puppy cannot see properly and finally not at all in the dark. Some breeds can be as much as three to five years before it manifests itself. The Irish Setter, however, can develop it quite young, but if tested and proved clear at the age of four months, it will not develop it. A simple test is to take your puppy into a strange place and note if he bumps into things as it grows dusk. It can also show signs of nervousness at dusk or in the dark, which it does not display during the day.

Some breeds are also being examined by their breeders for Hip Displasia which can be very painful and cause permanent lameness; it is

also a hereditary disease and not apparent in a baby puppy. Both these must indicate how important it is to buy from a breeder.

**FEEDING.** It is impossible to give exact amounts for every breed owing to their variation in size, plus the fact that like men each dog will vary in the amount he will require. You can only be guided by his condition. If he gets thin after you buy him, then increase the amount and vice versa. A rough quick guide is as follows:

A 10 pound dog requires $\frac{1}{2}$lb food per day.

A 25 pound dog requires $1\frac{1}{2}$lbs food per day.

A 40 pound dog requires $1\frac{3}{4}$lbs food per day.

Bear in mind at least half of this should be *protein*, in other words, meat or fish. The rest should be carbohydrates such as biscuit meal or brown bread. As a puppy the golden rule is 'little and often'. At the age of eight weeks to three months a puppy should have four meals a day at roughly four hour intervals. Two meals, generally the second and fourth, should consist of meat or fish and brown bread or biscuit meal – the latter scalded, but not made sloppy with good stock or Marmite gravy (which is very good for him). The other two meals should be milk and cereal. At the age of three months to six months he should have three meals at roughly six hour intervals. Still keep to the two meat and biscuit meals and leave out the second milk meal. When he is aged six months to twelve months, two meals should be sufficient with a handful of hard rusks or biscuits to go to bed with.

As this book deals with puppies, it must be explained that like babies it is important they are given added vitamins in their food. There are many preparations on the market which will tell you they are complete and nothing extra is necessary. There are breeders who use them in their kennels, with no doubt good results, but they are dealing with numbers and it makes feeding easy just to put down a bowl of dry biscuit and a dish of water. They are kennel dogs and do not know about juicy red beef or the taste of chicken which you with your one or even two puppies can give. Chicken is cheaper than beef these days and very nourishing for a small puppy, particularly one of the Toy breeds. Incidentally these 'Toys' should not be given sloppy food in the mistaken idea that their teeth are unable to cope with dry food. It can well be that much of the trouble with teeth in these small breeds is because they are given too moist foods. Their meals should be given just the same as any other breed. The biscuit should be scalded and covered over to steam, with any running gravy poured away. There are varying grades of Kibbled meal and the wholemeal plain one is the best.

The vitamins most necessary at

*A proud Pekinese and her puppy. This Pekinese puppy has not yet grown his full lion-like main and flowing coat and has an almost 'clipped' look.*

first are A and D which promote growth and resistance to disease. Vitamins B, C, and E are also necessary in helping to prevent skin trouble and the latter is a guard against sterility. Halibut Oil capsules are good and can be given with bone meal. Ask the breeder for a feeding chart which will then help you over the amounts to give. You can of course use a compound of all the vitamins and there are several products on the market which may be less trouble for you, but will be more expensive. If you give your puppy milk, eggs, meat and fish mixed with

biscuit or brown bread he will be getting a balanced diet.

Of the various fish, herrings are a wonderful food as they contain so many nutriments including iodine, which is very beneficial especially to the big breeds. Just put them in a saucepan of cold water and bring them to the boil, no more. Then take them out by the tail, give them a little shake and all the flesh will come off the main backbone (the smaller side bones do not matter). Puppies usually adore them mixed with crumbled brown bread. If circumstances make it necessary for you to change

*Above, a Cocker Spaniel puppy just arrived at his new home.*

*Top right, Border Terriers are delightful pets. They are small and the harsh coat needs no trimming while their 'flap-over' velvet-like ears give them extra charm. Their size is deceptive as they have forceful characters and are very strong with an amazing amount of energy; they can however be relied upon to be gentle with the family.*

*Right, St Bernards searching for the last scraps of food.*

the diet, do it gradually, mixing the old with the new. Strangely a change of water can sometimes cause an upset tummy in a baby puppy, if you suspect this, give it boiled for a while; also boiled milk can help with these little upsets.

Just in case you do not get an itemized diet sheet here are three examples for an eight-week-old puppy. Remember of course that the amounts must be increased as he grows. This may sound obvious but new owners who are carefully following a diet sheet may forget.

Bitch milk is much stronger than cow's milk, being richer in calcium; but goat's milk is also strong and is better than anything other than mum, if you can get it. Therefore, feed your puppy until he is at least three months of age on any of the prepared puppy milk foods. After three months he can go on to cow's milk with honey added, which is better than glucose and very popular with most puppies. In case of sickness honey and boiled water is a wonderful medicine to help recovery; also barley water is excellent for puppies with upset 'tums'. Orange juice, tomatoes, raw minced carrot (this is particularly beneficial) and parsley all help to make for a healthy lively puppy, but cooked vegetables are useless.

**Diet for puppies eight weeks old weighing under ten pounds when adult:**

8 am    1–2ozs milk (Lactol) thickened with Farex or brown bread and half a teaspoon of honey.

Midday  1–2ozs raw, finely minced lean meat with 1 dessertspoon to 1 tablespoon puppy meal and add vitamin compounds.

4 pm    Repeat the early morning meal and add an egg.

8–9 pm  Repeat the midday meal without the vitamins.

*Left, 'the eight weeks puppy is generally a good traveller'.*
*Top right, Cocker Spaniel pup.*
*Right, Lhasa Apso family.*
*Following pages: top left, Bearded Collie bitch and her puppy.*
*Below, a family of Golden Retrievers.*
*Right, Alsatian puppies are nearly always dark when they are young.*

*Above, Labradors are among the top six most popular breeds.*
*Top left, Samoyeds playing.*
*Left, Foxhound pups in kennels.*

**Diet for puppies eight weeks old weighing ten to twelve pounds when adult:**

Follow the preceding diet but increase the amounts by about a third.

**Diet for puppies eight weeks old weighing twenty to thirty pounds when adult:**

8 am    $\frac{1}{4}$–$\frac{1}{2}$ pint warm milk food with Farex or brown bread and 1 teaspoon honey added.

Midday    A small handful of puppy meal scalded with stock or Marmite but not made sloppy. Add 2ozs raw, minced meat, fish or chicken, 1 teaspoon carrot, Vivomin or 1 halibut oil capsule and $\frac{1}{2}$–$\frac{3}{4}$ teaspoon calcium Lactate.

4 pm    Repeat the early morning meal, add raw egg three to four times weekly.

8–9 pm    Repeat the midday meal but delete the additives.

Some charcoal biscuits or baked brown bread rusk may be given to go to bed with.

**Diet for puppies eight weeks old weighing thirty pounds and upwards when adult:**

8 am    $\frac{1}{2}$–$\frac{3}{4}$ pint warm milk food with Farex or 3–6 slices of brown bread broken up and 1 teaspoonful honey.

Midday    6ozs–$\frac{1}{2}$lb raw or cooked meat chopped in small pieces, or fish. Add 3–4 handfuls of puppy meal scalded as in previous diets. Add vitamin compounds with 2 halibut oil capsules, 1 teaspoon to 1 dessertspoon bone meal or calcium lactate, carrot, etc.

4 pm    Repeat the morning meal and add an egg.

8–9 pm    Repeat the midday meal without the additives.

Hard rusks or biscuits to go to bed with.

These menus are only a rough guide, since the amounts will vary slightly according to the individual puppies and breeds.

# Whelping and weaning

*A family of Whippets.*

# the puppies

This chapter might perhaps have come first but it really is essential you should know how to look after and feed a weaned puppy before you take on whelping a bitch. As previously mentioned you can expect your bitch to have her first season about eight to nine months of age.

It is not usual to mate her at the first season. However, should she not have it until she is, say, eleven months old, and if this coincides with the spring, there is no harm in mating her at this time. She will be thirteen months old before the puppies arrive and if she is slow in developing her body and ribs this will help her to do so.

In the case of a very young bitch choose an experienced dog as opposed to one of her own age. The stud dog has nothing at all to do with the number of puppies in the litter. This is controlled by the bitch, and depends entirely on the number of eggs she lets down at the time of the mating which are then fertilized by the dog. For this reason if the bitch is ready and willing, and not of the waspish turn of mind, do let her play with the dog beforehand. She will be much more likely to conceive, as she will relax and more eggs will be released for fertilization. It is quite easy to see if she is a willing bride without any danger to the stud dog.

To ascertain if a bitch is ready, which is normally at the tenth or twelfth day, you can stroke the root of her tail, or even examine her hindquarters, and she will move her tail from one side to another. If you have another bitch with her the fact that they will often fool about together is really no indication that she is ready for mating, as they often do this from the first day she started her season.

There are some bitches who will always resent being mated and these must be held, to prevent their really

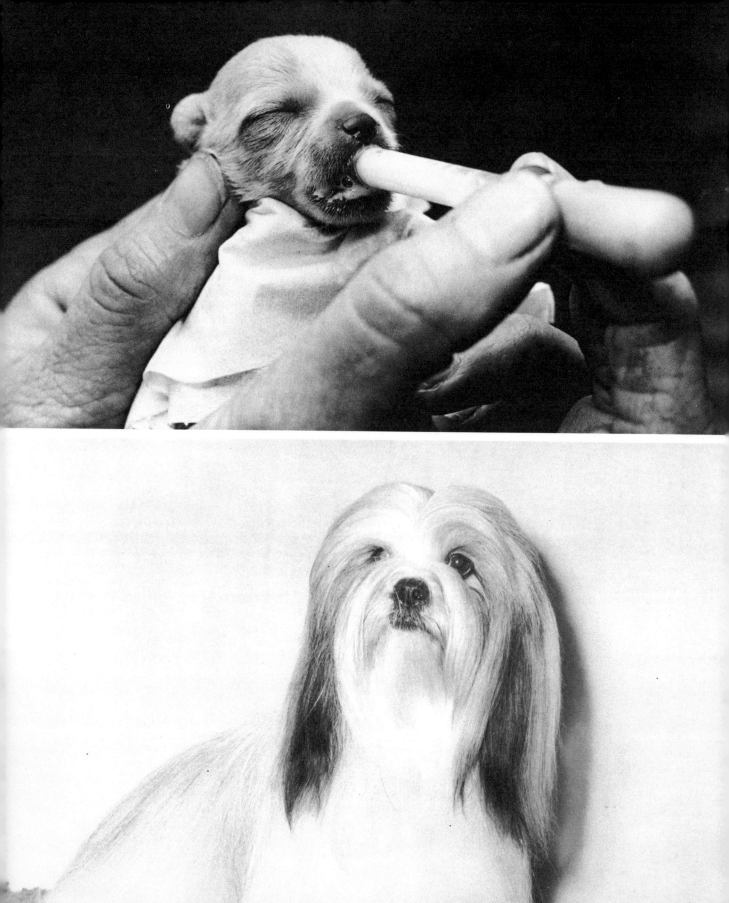

turning on the dog. A bandage wound round the muzzle has a most calming effect. They realize that once this has been applied they are not in a position to bite, and cease to protest, so that the mating proceeds in the normal way. There is nothing cruel in this.

Do not insist on being present at the mating. Having seen the stud dog, make yourself scarce once the dogs have been introduced, and ask the owner if you may see the 'tie'. This will be suggested, as being more satisfactory to you both. The bitch will be better without your presence and so will the stud dog and his owner. A troublesome bitch is always better without her owner. Let her rest a bit before the return journey and keep her quiet for a few days after the mating, without violent exercise.

Your bitch should finish her season about three weeks from its start. Her being mated makes no difference to the length of it. The fact that she may go on showing the coloured discharge for some time after the mating is no indication of her having 'missed', as is sometimes thought. It is however noticeable that a bitch in whelp never quite dries up completely. She remains slightly moist and wet during

the nine weeks of her pregnancy.

Many books will tell you to worm your bitch after mating, which is a most dangerous practice. This should have been done beforehand, about a month before she was due in season.

From the time she comes in season until the time you are sure she is in whelp, she will benefit from the addition of some wheat germ. This is the vitamin E which stimulates the reproductive organs. The directions on the packet give the amount. She will not require any addition to her normal diet until three weeks before whelping. She should however have at least half a pound of meat a day during the entire time.

During the last two weeks she should go on to two meals a day:

**Morning meal**
$\frac{1}{2}$ pint milk and 1 egg with wheatgerm. Add 1 teaspoon honey and $\frac{1}{2}$ small teaspoon bicarbonate of soda. The latter will prevent any acidity in the milk when she whelps. The honey takes the bitter taste away.

**Main meal at 5–6 pm**
Give $\frac{3}{4}$ to 1lb meat according to her appearance. If she looks as though she is going to have a great many puppies the latter amount will not be too much. Add to this 2 halibut oil capsules and 1 calcium tablet during the last 2 weeks.

When she has been mated three or four weeks, a vet can generally tell you if she is in whelp, as the embryo can be felt by an experienced person.

Do be sure the bitch has plenty of exercise, but on no account allow her to run up and down stairs after the third week. This can cause the death of the puppies, or at least some of them. Be sure she is free from lice and fleas. Give her a good dusting with an insect powder, but do not bath her after five or six weeks unless she is used to it. A pet who is used to the car every day can continue her rides, but not a kennel dog, as she will not be used to them.

At the last week cut away the hair from around her teats, and wash them well. Also trim her hind feathering with the trimming scissors. You will not want to cut this away in case of spoiling her looks. Wash this well, also her hindquarters. This should be done again on the 58th and 59th days.

The time given for a bitch to carry her puppies is 60 to 63 days. Many have them on the 60th day. If you have any reason to think a bitch is going to whelp, an infallible guide is to take her temperature, and if it is normal she is foxing you. The temperature always drops to below 100° twelve hours before whelping. This has been proved over and over again. So if you think of staying up at night, take her temperature last thing. This will be your guide. You will want to be with her, and as a rule she will give you warning that she would like her 'hand held'. Some bitches will eat a hearty meal and then suddenly start in labour, but usually they will give some sign.

*Top left, the size of this tiny Chihuahua puppy can be seen against the hand that is holding him. He is being fed with a pen filler.*
*Left, a Shih Tzu.*
*Below, a Pekinese puppy longing for a game.*

The question of where the maternity ward is to be must be decided by you early in her pregnancy, as the bitch must get used to it some time before she whelps. The quarters must have some sort of heating as newly born puppies must have warmth. More litters are lost through the lack of it than anything else. If she is to be in a kennel it is not expensive to run an electric light to it and install an infra red lamp. The best ones cost very little, and have a bulb of 250 watts which has a red glass round it. This throws the heat down on to the box, and has not the bright light of the kind supplied for chicken rearing. There is also what is called a 'dull emitter', which is good for heating a kennel in winter, but it is general heating, and not directed downwards, which is the point of the infra red lamp. This keeps the bed warm and dry, and also dries the puppies as they arrive. It should be hung about three feet from the floor of the box, but can be altered according to the behaviour of the bitch. Should you decide to have her indoors, which is best, choose a place where she will be undisturbed and not have her nerves continually on edge with people coming in and out.

Lastly, the bed. The best for this would be a box with high sides and back, the top of which can be covered over with a lid or blanket. Until the 59th or 60th day the usual straw can be used as bedding if she is in a kennel, or a blanket if she is in the house. After this time a good supply of small pieces of torn newspaper, about six inches square, should replace them. This makes the best and cleanest bed for the whelping, and one which she will enjoy tearing up. The puppies cannot get lost under it, as in the case of the straw or blanket. Give her plenty and do not stint it.

You should be equipped with the following:

A thermometer
Cotton wool
A weak solution of permanganate of potash
A small cardboard box, large enough to take a hot-water bottle wrapped in a piece of blanket
Two or three small towels
Vaseline

*Staffordshire Bull Terrier puppies.*

108

The normal whelping is really a most thrilling and exciting experience, and every litter born has the same thrill to it. But for you at your first it may hold moments of acute alarm. Most bitches know exactly what to do and if you just sit by her she will be grateful for your presence. On no account give her any food, either just before or during her whelping, unless it is very protracted, when a small drink of warm milk can be given. This is because you do not want to overload the bladders, which then presses against the uterus, and can hold up the birth of the puppies. Do not interfere with her when she starts scratching up the papers, and throwing them all over the place. This is natural to her in her instinct to make a bed and once this has started, don't let her out of the kennel (if that is where she is) unless on a lead. She may disappear underneath it and have her puppies there, a highly disconcerting process, and one not unknown to breeders. One of them had to have the entire floor taken up in the middle of the night to get at a bitch who had done exactly this.

Sometimes the sight of the first puppy upsets a bitch, and she will refuse to have anything to do with it. Then you must quickly clear its head free from the bag in which every puppy is born. It is clear, like cellophane, and at the first glance you might not notice that the puppy is enclosed in it. Once it is born it will suffocate unless freed quickly. If the afterbirth is still attached to the puppy, sever this with some blunt scissors, about an inch away from its body, and with a warm towel rub it dry. This you can do quite briskly to make it cry and draw breath in its lungs. At the sound of its voice the bitch will probably realize what it is all about, and get agitated, so quickly put it back with her, and encourage her to lick it and so stimulate it into life. Until the second one arrives, which is generally fairly quickly, she may continue to be rather stupid about the first one, but as the new arrivals appear she will settle down to the job and give no further bother.

If, however, there is any undue delay between the puppies, and the bitch does a lot of straining with no result, it is advisable to call the vet, as there may be something wrong. On the other hand, if she is just sleeping between having puppies and is not distressed, leave her alone and let her rest. Should she rest too long, say more than two or three hours, it is as well to get her up and perhaps take her out on the lead for a moment. This will start things going again.

In the case of a large litter, the early arrivals can be moved to the warmth of another box with a hot-water bottle, to be thoroughly dried off under the blanket. Remove each one whilst she is busy with the next, and replace it also when she is otherwise occupied.

Each puppy will have an afterbirth attached, which it is normal for the mother to eat when detaching the puppy from the navel cord. Sometimes it comes with the puppy and sometimes after. It is most important that you should know that one has been passed for each puppy. One left behind can cause septicaemia or blood-poisoning, resulting in the death of the bitch. If you have any doubts ring your vet and tell him, as it must be dealt with at once. The womb contracts anything from twenty to twenty-four hours after the whelping, so quick action is obviously necessary.

The completion of the whelping can generally be told by the relaxed and peaceful condition of the bitch, who will stretch herself out and give a big sigh, as much as to say 'Well, that's that!' At this stage you should quietly remove all the soiled pieces of paper that remain. Replace them with dry ones, and continue with the paper for the next three days. Then if she is quite peaceful and quiet with the puppies, give her a blanket. Some

*The Finnish Spitz is a northern dog whose foxy appearance is enhanced by the reddish colour of his coat. They have charming characters however.*

bitches will scratch the blanket into a heap, thereby smothering the puppies, hence the reason for the continuation of the paper.

Once you think she has finished offer her a bowl of half a pint of warm milk boiled and thickened with one teaspoonful of honey, half a teaspoonful of bicarbonate of soda and one heaped teaspoonful of Lactogol (milk stimulant) sold by the chemist in capsules, not to be confused with the Puppy Milk Food. You will probably have to hold her food bowl for her to feed for a few days, as she will be so proud of her family, she will not want to come out of her box, even for food. Her diet for the next twenty-four hours should be a milky one, giving her the Lactogol – as sold for the

*Salukis . . . these are the hounds of the desert and they were bred for hunting gazelle. Like Greyhounds they have excellent eyesight. They are very beautiful dogs with gentle natures.*

human nursing mother – three times a day. This is a powerful milk stimulant and an excellent preparation for the encouraging of milk in bitches. Continue with it during her lactation.

After the second day she should be fed three or four times daily, according to the size of her litter. Her food should include one pound of raw meat and one pint of milk every day, according to breed and size. Remember that the raw meat is important, as it helps to make her milk more than the milk diet does. That only supplies the liquid intake. Continue with the bicarbonate of soda while she is nursing the puppies.

After the third day, let her have plenty of exercise. This stimulates her and the milk glands. If you notice any puppy not getting on or sucking properly, pinch its skin up between your thumb and forefinger, and if it does not spring back almost at once, that puppy is not thriving. You can help it get a stronger hold on life by giving it a little extra nourishment from a bottle three times a day.

There is one feeder on the market, the Belcroy from Bell and Croydon, London, which is for premature babies. It is like a very large fountain-pen filler, with a teat at both ends. The smaller one has a hole in it, which will have to be slightly enlarged for a puppy by pushing a darning needle, previously made red hot, into the existing hole. If the puppy is too weak to suck you can pinch the large teat and a little milk will be squirted into the puppy's mouth, which will probably start it sucking. The glass phial is marked in teaspoons, so that you can see how much the puppy is taking. For the mixture you should follow the directions on the tin of Lactol Puppy Food, sold at pet shops. The mixture needs to be really warm when put in the feeder. Puppies hate a lukewarm bottle, and will take it far hotter than you would imagine – a little warmer than blood heat.

At four days old the short tailed breeds should have their tails cut and dew claws removed. The latter are

generally only confined to the front legs, but some puppies have them on the hind paws as well. Be sure to keep an eye on them in case the bleeding starts again. If it does dab the end with permanganate crystals. Of course, the mother should be removed out of earshot beforehand. She can return five or ten minutes after the operation.

While the bitch is nursing her puppies, see they do not make her sore with their sharp little nails. If they do, snip a little off the ends with a pair of curved nail scissors.

**WEANING THE PUPPIES.** This should start at three and a half to four weeks, according to the size of the litter, by giving them a teaspoonful of scraped, lean, fresh raw meat, made by scraping shin of beef with a spoon. This is far easier and works much better than using a knife, and you do not cut yourself! Puppies may be rather foolish at first, but once they realize how good it is there will be a scrimmage to be first. Feed each one separately. Continue this for three days, and then give it twice daily. This will take them to four and half or five weeks old, and they can be promoted to milk foods, goat's milk and Lactol Puppy milk food. If this makes them at all loose in their insides, add one tablespoon of Kaolin powder per five puppies to the milk powder, and mix in the usual way.

After five weeks they can have barley kernels added, rice pudding, semolina, etc. The diet can be just the same as that for the eight week pet puppy, but do not add the biscuit meal before the age of seven weeks. At this age they should be wormed. Therefore ask your vet for the newest remedy, making sure to mention the age and breed.

It is a good thing to sell your surplus puppies at about eight weeks of age. It is no good hanging on to them with the mistaken idea you will get more when they are older. You will probably feel uncertain in your own mind, but it is better to sell them young than find yourself with a lot of puppies you cannot sell, as they are past the 'pretty' stage.

Do not on any account overfeed the litter at any time. Always feed them in separate dishes placed well apart. Some will eat faster than others and if near together they can easily nip in and steal from the slow ones. This should be a golden rule right from the first. Also no titbits between meals. It is important not to allow any breed to become fat, especially the big breeds as they can so easily go crooked on their legs if their bodies become too heavy before the bone has hardened.

The big hounds and guard dog breeds grow very quickly, so it is most essential you do not forget their

vitamins and calcium. If by any chance one does seem to be getting too fat, cut down on his biscuit meal and bread rather than on his meat, milk or eggs.

Milk is very good for puppies but some of them do go off it, in which case, whilst still giving him the necessary number of meals for his age, disguise it, if he is not too fat, by adding more bread which will make it less liquid in form. The Farex Baby Food can sometimes bore even the small puppy, so give him Weetabix instead, it has more substance to it. Farex need really be only a 'starter' at the early weaning time.

On no account let any puppy rush madly about immediately after feeding; certainly put him out to relieve himself but let him rest after food. All puppies need plenty of sleep and they should have a special pen where they can be left in peace, not only to digest their food but to grow too. The big-framed dogs should never be allowed to tear about playing together after food. Many breeds such as

*Below, Beagles are some of the most appealing puppies of all, but it must not be forgotten that they are pack animals and will need a lot of exercise when they are older, once they have been trained not to run after every animal within sight or sound! Right, French Bulldog puppies.*

Borzois, Deerhounds, Irish Wolfhounds, Bloodhounds, are prone to what is known as 'Distension'. This is a build-up of gas in the stomach which must have immediate attention by a vet. Violent exercise after food, with the twisting and turning that the bigger breeds indulge in at play, may not directly be the cause, but it may well help to induce this very often fatal condition.

These breeds can benefit from having their feeding dishes put up on a box, say about a foot high as they grow older. This applies especially to the long necked and long legged hounds. It can help to keep their shoulders and fronts correct, should you have any idea of showing.

Just remember you have a new puppy, all legs and tail. He is a bundle of energy, no doubt noisy and awkward and untrained. His future progress, his behaviour and subsequent health and temperament will be entirely up to you. He will go through all kinds of difficult stages during his development, not only in growth but also in character.

At times he will aggravate you almost beyond endurance, the next moment he will enchant you with his winning ways. He will try and do his best for you but he is young and much of the world around him is still incomprehensible. He will love you whatever you do and ask for nothing but your love (and food) in return. He may chew up your favourite warm slippers, but you will never be lonely if you have a dog which you have trained and loved since puppyhood.

# Exercising and showing

From an early age your puppy should have space in which to play, and if you have only one try and play with him. At eight weeks just a little pen is sufficient – you can make him an excellent one by buying some of the plastic covered panels which are sold at the Garden Centres for surrounding compost beds. They are neat and you can make the pen any size you need, as they are about three feet high by approximately four to six feet long. Of course the big breeds will try and jump out but at first these panels will be a boon to you. If it is summer time put a box inside for him to sleep in and of course do not have it out in the blazing sun.

*Right, a Shih Tzu and her fluffy puppy. These dogs are recognized in America, though not yet in England. Their origin is probably Chinese and like the other Chinese breeds they have the snub nose and often a comical awareness of their own self-importance and dignity.*

*Below, a Dalmatian puppy taking itself for a walk.*

Do not force him to go for walks on a road until he is at least four months old, when you have got him lead trained, and then only for a period of 20 minutes or so. Take him in a quiet road at first until he is used to the odd car, though by now he should be car-trained if you have been taking him out with you. As he gets older increase the distance and when you think he is quite nerve free and unmoved by noises, take him into the shops with you. This is particularly valuable if you want to show him later on.

From six to eight months of age onwards, he should have regular road exercise, especially if he is going to grow large. About 30 to 40 minutes should be about right. He should also have a free galloping period, either

# a puppy

in a large paddock or out with you in the fields. Do not overdo this with the big hounds and do give him regular rest periods every day. Shut him away where he has to sleep and can not jump up at every noise he hears. A good time for this is after his midday meal, and at least two hours is a good idea. He will of course sleep at other times during the day, but this set rest period should be a part of his training. Greyhound trainers always do this and the hounds are put away where there is not even a window that they can jump up at to look out. This may not be so important for your little dog, but it is a must for those who will grow to be 22 inches or more when they are adult.

Quite a good way to exercise the big hounds is to put them on a lead and take them out with a bicycle. This must be with a responsible person who will not run him too fast. The pace must only be a brisk trot or fast walk and he must not go before he is eight to nine months old. This will help greatly to strengthen his hindquarters and back muscles. A weakness in these regions is often the cause of bad action in the show ring.

Do not take him on any long walks if he shows any weakness or signs of rickets in his front legs; you will notice this if he stands badly in front. Let your vet see him if he displays a 'Charlie Chaplin' front when he is about four months old. He can be given injections to help this, plus perhaps extra calcium or a change of diet. You may have been giving him everything quite correctly but some youngsters do not absorb the right amount of calcium.

It is not nearly so easy to rear a big fellow such as a Great Dane as it is to raise the smaller puppy. The breeder can help you a great deal in the very important age group of three to nine months of age. If in doubt do keep in touch and ask for advice. They will be as anxious as you that the puppy should prove to be a success, especially if you have bought it for show.

It very often happens that a puppy sold as a pet may display show potential as he reaches maturity, and your knowledgeable friends may say that you ought to show him. You then take him along to the local charity show which puts on classes for dogs. If you have trained him

correctly and he walks and stands as you have taught him, you may win a card or a rosette, and believe it or not you are 'hooked' on the show game. It goes to your head like champagne and the following week you will be trying to find the date of the next show.

These charity shows accept all breeds and ages of dogs, but the Kennel Club shows are confined to dogs of six months and over. In other countries, such as America, they have special baby puppy classes which are great fun. However, the English take things more seriously, thinking in their wisdom that a puppy should not be subject to the excitement of a show ring before he is six months. Maybe they are right.

This is certainly true of the big dogs. Classes are planned for puppies of six to nine months and puppies six to twelve months of age. It stands to reason that a baby of only six months cannot hope to compete against one of nine months old. Whilst he may behave perfectly, he has not the maturity, size or substance in body to beat the older puppy. You may like to get him used to the excitement of a show, but do not expect great things. If he is of the hound variety just be happy with him if he stands up and moves with confidence. This is excellent.

It is quite different with the smaller breeds that mature quickly. For instance it is possible that one of only nine months can go right to the top and win the whole show, beating champions in the process, but do not expect this of the big breed puppy. It is better that he does not mature

*Right, a Yorkshire Terrier puppy which is obviously destined for the show ring.*
*Below, very young Bloodhound puppies which have not yet developed the dome-shaped head and the portentous frowns of their parents.*

*Top left, 'Expectant Mum' obviously fed up with the whole situation – or is it a Basset playing to the gallery again?*

*Left, weeks later, the puppies all feeding out of individual bowls in the garden.*

*Above, a twelve week old Jack Russell Terrier with rather over-large ears. These are very popular dogs which are not yet recognized by the Kennel Clubs, though they have won more support than some of their more exotic pedigree relatives.*

too quickly otherwise he may not grow to the right height. Give him time and if you must show him, confine your outings to the small local show to give him confidence and learn what is expected of him.

You too must be sure of yourself and confident that you are presenting him correctly. Many owners are nervous in the show ring and this is sensed by the dog – your nerves can travel down that lead like electricity and suddenly, for no apparent reason, the puppy that walked so well in the town and behaved perfectly towards

strangers in the shops is lying flat on the ground and refusing to move at all. If you have trained him and you know he is reliable, this behaviour can be your fault, not his. So take a hold on yourself, remember that everyone is looking at your dog, not you. Talk to your puppy just as you would at home. Pat him, encourage him and standing up straight say in an ordinary happy way 'Come on, let's go' and nine times out of ten he will. A nervous, unhappy, 'creepy' owner makes for an unhappy 'creepy' puppy. They are most responsive to your voice so do not be afraid to use it. Just a soft tone is sufficient.

The professional handlers are a great example of this mutual confidence. It is very unusual to see them showing a shy puppy. You may think this is because they have given it ring training, but this is not so. It will have been taught to go on a collar and lead the same as your pet and possibly learnt the command to 'stand'. In many cases they may not even have met until the day of the show. It is because the 'Pro' loves animals. He has great understanding, he is able to give the puppy the reassurance it needs.

There are certain formalities that must be carried out before you can show any puppy at a Kennel Club show. It has to be registered with them (this is not necessary at the exemption or local show), although if you have bought from a breeder it is very likely to be named already, in which case you will have been given its Kennel Club registration card. With it you should also have a Kennel Club transfer form. This you will have to complete and send up with the appropriate fee; you will then receive another card from them confirming that the puppy is transferred to you and registered in your name.

The exemption and local shows have no formalities for entering their classes, in fact you can just turn up on the day and go in for whatever appeals to you. There are generally four classes for pedigree dogs and puppies, several others are provided such as 'the dog the judge would like to take home', which is then judged on the one which most appeals to the judge irrespective of its show points. There may be one for 'The Dog in Best Condition' often judged by a vet. You could be in a good position if it happened to be your vet, and your dog was in really good form. Be

*Sealyham Terriers were deliberately created in the 19th century to be badger dogs, and as these puppies show, they have great charm and also a good sense of humour.*

sure its teeth are sparkling white for this class. At one such show the vet went round every dog opening its mouth and just saying 'dirty teeth' and passing on to the next, being finally left with three puppies who were so young that no tartar had collected on their teeth.

It is important for show that the teeth should not have a tartar deposit on them. It is important anyway for the sake of the dog. Therefore, if this does form despite your care pay a visit to your vet and let him deal with it for you.

It is as well to remember that the entries for a Kennel Club show close some time ahead and you should send for a schedule from the Secretary. Your friend the breeder can help you as regards the best classes to enter. It would be wise to pay a visit to a few shows and watch the procedure before you finally enter at one. At the big championship shows, such as Crufts which you will certainly know about, your dog is allotted what is known as a bench. This is a raised platform which is partitioned off at either side with galvanized iron, so that he cannot either 'smell noses' or be 'attacked' by his next door neighbour. It is about two feet from the ground and the width is according to his size. There is a hook at the rear to which he must be attached by a chain, not a leather lead as if he hates the whole affair he will quickly chew through this and be off if you leave him. Anyway you would not want to leave him, as you must be sure he is not going to fret and try to strangle himself in the event of the chain being too long. Take a nice blanket or rug for him to lie on, also two bowls, one for food which you must take with you, just a small amount of something he really likes, and one for water. Take a bottle of milk and a bottle of water, as even if he does not want food he may enjoy the milk. Though there will be a water tap around the show somewhere, it is much easier to have your own in a handy bottle.

The thrill of winning your first prize, winning that first red card, is a moment you will never forget, even though you may win bigger rewards later on. In other countries blue is generally given as the first prize; English judges going overseas are often very startled when mistakenly they hand out the Red Ribbon to the winner, who draws back in horror thinking he has not won after all.

*Right, Pharaoh Hound and puppies.*
*Below, three Whippet puppies.*

# Puppies around the world

There is no doubt that the English are great Dog lovers, but they are by no means the only ones. I would say they are way behind America, whose Kennel Club premises in New York must be the finest in the world. The club occupies several storeys of a magnificent building, and the corridors are lined with beautiful pictures of dogs by the old Masters. Its library has every book on the subject that you can think of and is available to dog breeders for interest and research. The pedigrees are done by computer and in one year alone they processed half a million Poodle pedigrees. It is a dog breeders' paradise. The Kennel Club is rightly proud of it and many groups of breeders are taken on conducted tours. The American Kennel Club was founded in 1895 just two years after the English Kennel Club.

*Above, the Tibetan Terrier is a breed which is still a rarity in the Western World though they are so attractive and hardy that it seems very likely that their numbers will increase.*

It is a splendid idea that in America, Canada and Australia there are shows of Futurity Stakes for Puppies only. These are grouped into ages and divided by sex. The age groups are two to four months, four to six months, six to nine months and finally nine to twelve months. In the States they draw entries from Canada and Alaska and from the West Coast as well as East.

There will be as many as a hundred puppies at these events in the more popular breeds. It is held by a Breed Club and the idea is not only to get the puppies used to shows but also to seek out the novices and newcomers. It is made into a social event as well as a dog show, and also encourages the junior handlers.

These puppy matches are great fun, and from them can come the future Champions. The puppies are a delightful sight, all of the same breed, generally in country surroundings with friends they know. Of course they hop and skip about, they sit down and even lie down, but it is all a great day out. It is laid on for those who breed dogs not only scientifically with a watchful eye for the right points in the breed, but also for those who love them as well, which should be the primary reason why dogs are bred at all.

Australia follows the same pattern. In this vast and on the whole sparsely populated country, dog owners think nothing of driving 500 miles to a dog

*Far page top, a Pekinese puppy ready for a game. Centre, young Papillons whose ears are not fully 'feathered'. These attractive toy dogs also have gorgeous plumed tails which curl over their backs. Bottom, is an older Chihuahua puppy of the smooth-haired variety. Right, an alert healthy Miniature Pinscher puppy. The outstanding characteristic of the 'Min Pin' is their hackney action.*

show. There are shows way out in the country where you can see classes of their Cattle Dogs, Australian Heelers, Blue Speckle Cattle Dogs and Queensland Heelers, not seen except in Australia. The cattleman relies on these for the protection of his sheep. Through years of selective breeding using Scotch collies they have now achieved a dog perfectly suited to the work they have to do. The 'Kelpie' which means Water Sprite in Gaelic, have the most fantastic intelligence and affection for their owners, coupled with devotion to duty. As puppies they are natural workers and there are no less than 70,000 to 80,000 Kelpies working in Australia now. It is said they can do the work of six men when getting the sheep penned.

Australian Terriers must not be forgotten. Their first Club was formed in 1889. Then called the Rough Coated Terrier it was not until 1909 that the word 'Australian' was added. Sandy Scotch Terriers were their background breed, and they are not unlike a Yorkshire Terrier in colouring, though bigger with a harsh coat. Very game, smart and alert, they make an ideal child's companion and house pet. They are full of character and are loyal and devoted.

There is a true story told of a shepherd whose sheepdog bitch had a litter aged a month old. He was short of manpower one day, and thinking the puppies old enough to be left on their own with his wife, he took the bitch to help him drive his flock to a town ten miles away, where they stayed the night. He settled both sheep and dogs, but when he went back later in the evening to see that all was well, he found the bitch had vanished. Meanwhile back home his wife went to feed the puppies and to her surprise found their mother busy feeding them, so left her with them. She realized the bitch had trotted the ten miles back after her day's work to feed her puppies, and did not expect her then to return to work. However when the shepherd went down in the morning there she was, having travelled through the night back to her master and her work.

They all start young. The Australian cattle dog puppy is taken out with his mother to let him see her working. Of course he gets in the way of the horse and often gets trodden on and so learns to keep behind. He gets in the way of his mother who nips him sharply to remind him not to interfere. He watches and learns, the instinct is there all the time. One day his instinct drives him to take a nip at the heels of a heifer. He does it with incredible speed and instantly flattens on the ground to avoid the almost as quick lash back of the heifer.

He has done exactly what he was bred for, and from that moment on though still a puppy he will work untiringly. At first he may refuse to return to the horse's heel, and one day he may get a bit too eager and receive a nasty kick, but if he is made of the right material he will regain his confidence and profiting by this very salutary lesson take greater care in future.

Border Collies do excellent obedience work in this country at shows, but more important still their breeders guard them most carefully for their working abilities. They are not recognized for shows here, but in Australia they have classes along with the other breeds. The puppies work naturally from an early age and put with another breed they can be watched rounding up the other puppies and circling them just as though they were sheep.

South Africa is another country that likes to encourage the 'young entry'. They schedule puppy classes to encourage the exhibitor, and as they are not able to have so many shows this is a great help to puppy owners. Just like the American and Australian puppy events, the South African classes have a good informal atmosphere.

The Breed Clubs in particular make a speciality of the relaxed and friendly feelings they try to maintain in these puppy matches and shows confined to the one breed. This also applies to the Clubs which specialize in Obedience and Ringcraft classes. The latter teach you how to train your puppy for showing. This should be the first step before you enter for the Obedience class, which can for some puppies have too dampening effect on their spirits so it is wiser to join the Ringcraft first.

South America, too, is very keen on showing dogs and has imported a great many. Whilst the actual running of their shows has a more leisurely approach, they take their wins or losses very seriously. They show their young puppies, but do not take the same trouble to train them

*Left, the intelligent and beautiful eyes of a Dachshund puppy.*
*Right, a Rottweiler puppy. When grown up he will be a substantial dog of about 25 to 27 inches in height, black in colour with well defined brown markings and a docked tail.*

or stand them up properly in the show manner. On the other hand they are mostly kept as house pets, and are used to people. The result is that they show happily, whoever handles them. It is somewhat difficult to judge them as they cavort about just as the spirit moves them, but the show is always great fun for everyone concerned.

The Continent and Scandinavia have very strict rulings as regards the showing of puppies. They cannot qualify for championship awards before a certain age, which is varied in the breeds according to their size when adult. These countries, as well as Australia, also have examinations for judges. These are very comprehensive, covering not only the points of the breeds but also their general structure.

Junior handling plays a very large part in the shows in the States and

quite rightly. After all it is the children who will eventually be the Judges and Exhibitors of the future. The Australians also put on handling classes for them at the two huge mammoth shows, Melbourne Royal and Sydney Royal, both of which run for ten days. However, it is the Americans who really put on the best spectacle. There are two age groups, eight to eleven and twelve to seventeen years. Various shows during the year have classes for them, the final competition being held at the very prestigious Westminster Show which is equivalent to Crufts. It is held in Madison Square Garden, New York. Each child must have won five first prizes in order to enter for this final event. The build up for this is tremendous, and on the first night twelve are picked out from these finalists but not placed in order of merit. They

*Above, a Steinbrach family.*
*Right, a Maltese puppy playing in a pile of leaves. He has not yet grown the long coat which makes these dogs so elegant.*

return to compete for the title of Junior Handler of the Year on the finals night. The judges are not just the Lady Mayoress or a prominent notability visiting the show as so often happens in other countries. They are licensed Kennel Club judges, who judge the way the child presents the dog and not the dog's show points.

It is a great sight and the way these children present their dogs is an object lesson to all. They do not overdo things, and each one is so good it is really only the smallest detail that divides the last four. On one occasion

130

*The Dandie Dinmont is another Terrier that has the character and energy of a much bigger dog and which deserves to be better known. The 'Top Knot' of silky hair in contrast to the short, crisp coat can be clearly seen in this picture as can the distinctive 'eyebrows' on the puppies.*

an eleven-year-old boy was left in the finals. The judge called him out with five very tall girls. His charge was a standard black and tan Dachshund, not an easy breed to present, but his handling was perfection and it was obvious the judge was very taken with his performance.

In the States the dogs do not move straight up and down but make what is called the 'L' – this means they

go up the ring, they turn smartly to the left, go across it, turn round retracing their tracks and then return in a straight line to the judge. This is not easy as the child has to remember to change his lead to his right hand when turning round. Some dogs do not like being led on the right, as of course they are always moved anticlockwise being led in the left hand. It must be remembered on no account

should the handler get between the dog and the judge.

Our hero did all this perfectly, as also did his dog. They had obviously practised this well, neither showed any sign of emotion. On the return, the child must stop a few feet from the judge and stand the dog without touching it. This also went well and he returned to his place at the end of the line. He then got down on his knees and proceeded to get the dog's feet in position, holding out its tail and tightening the lead on its neck to get the head in position. Everyone was watching him but he was quite oblivious. Unfortunately he was so engrossed he failed to notice the judge had returned to him, and went on handling the dog which he should not have done when the judge was actually looking at it. This lost him a high place, but when the judge called him out to fourth place, his joy was unbounded. He swept the dog up into his arms, he laughed and he cried, he kissed it, he hugged it. The winner was splendid, it was very fair judging and everyone appreciated that she deserved to win. The boy did too. Having got over his first excitement he was about to leave the ring, then suddenly remembered, about turned and went back to shake her hand.

Sportsmanship is what dog show-showing can teach the children. This eleven-year-old boy had won five times during the year to get to Westminster and if he did feel a twinge of disappointment he certainly did not show it. This is how it should be. Children should learn from the very first moment a puppy comes into their lives that it is a pet, for which they are responsible, whether it wins or not. It loves them just the same, as they should love it.

It is to be hoped that parents who buy a puppy for the children buy one that is suitable for them. They should also not be too young when they have that first pet. It should also be explained to them and enforced if necessary that they do not pick it up and race it around on a lead all day long. It must be explained that a puppy needs its rest periods, just as they did when they were small. Do make a firm rule about this from the first. It is not an inanimate object or a toy to be discarded when they get

bored with it. If they have a puppy do make them take a share in looking after its needs.

What must be avoided at all costs is an attitude like that of one mother who at Christmas went to a famous kennel saying she wanted a puppy for the children. The owner asked her how many children there were and their ages as she did not really like selling a puppy to a household where there were several small children. The mother replied 'Oh, you need not worry about it, because when they